Shared
Vision

Norm Coleman and the Remarkable Revitalization of St. Paul

Introduction by John Labosky, president and CEO, Capital City Partnership

Edited by Tom Mason

**MASON
SMILEY
LARSON**
BOOKS

St. Paul, Minnesota

570 Asbury St., Suite 203
St. Paul, MN 55104

Designed by Scott Buchschacher

Cover photography by Anthony Brett Schreck

Interior photography by Aaron Smith

Printed in the United States of America

ISBN 1-931646-28-7

TABLE OF CONTENTS

Editor's Note 6

Introduction..10

Chapter 1: CEOs: Norm Coleman's Executive Operation 17

Chapter 2: River of Dreams.......................................32

Chapter 3: Building Blocks 51

Chapter 4: Slap Shot 62

Chapter 5: Cultural Renaissance................................75

Chapter 6: A Community Effort 86

Chapter 7: City Living...99

Chapter 8: Recreating Retail....................................110

Chapter 9: The City Goes to Market...........................125

Chapter 10: Future Visions 136

Chapter 11: Q&A: Norm Coleman 148

Editor's Note

I first met Norm Coleman six years ago while researching an article for *Twin Cities Business Monthly* about his vision to transform the economy of St. Paul. This kind of story can be easy to write, because most politicians are thrilled to fill reporters' notebooks with pithy gems about their grand vision for the future. But to be credible, a serious reporter will try to separate political happy talk from things that might actually take place.

From my first interview with the mayor, I had a sense that his were not empty words.

Coleman understood the strengths of the city and what needed to be done to exploit its potential. He emphasized the value of building upon St. Paul's historic neighborhoods and of making them safe, livable, and affordable. The city's economic base, he said, should not be limited to the borders of St. Paul, but should extend throughout the entire east metro, all the way to the Wisconsin border, and include flourishing suburbs like Woodbury and Eagan. And most important, he envisioned St. Paul as a reawakened river city in which culture, entertainment, commercial real estate, retail, and housing would all grow and evolve in a symbiotic connection to the Mighty Mississippi.

As I listened to him, I had no doubt Coleman would sell his

plan. St. Paul was littered with the well-placed words of politicians who failed to connect their high ideals and slick speeches to any kind of accomplishments. How much he would accomplish remained to be seen, but I knew his attempt to pull it off would be fun to watch. Coleman's 16-hour workdays and unwavering self-confidence were legendary, especially among staffers who had to try to keep up with him. I conducted more than 50 interviews for the story and could not find anyone who hadn't been touched by Coleman's hypnotic enthusiasm. There evidently wasn't a meeting he wouldn't attend, a question he wouldn't answer, or an interview he wouldn't grant. He would take risks when he had to, he'd say, and he wouldn't measure the value of a project by how popular it appeared in opinion polls. "Good policy will lead to good politics," became his mantra.

Writing for a business magazine, I was impressed by the urgency with which he reached out to the business community. "We can't do this without business," he said. Under the mentorship of Doug Leatherdale, CEO of The St. Paul Companies, and others, the mayor quickly grasped the value that business executives place on personal relationships. He methodically reached out to the city's business leaders at every level, seeking their input and asking for help. He hosted his share of formal meetings with them, but mostly he had breakfasts, lunches, and dinners. From the CEOs of large companies, he solicited personal advice. What does it take to run a large organization? How can I streamline my operation? How can I make it more efficient? How can I make it more responsive to the community? Many executives, surprised to finally meet a mayor from St. Paul, were delighted to respond.

I submitted an article of 5,000 words, about twice as long as I had expected it to be.

This book chronicles how he did it. It shows what can be achieved when a visionary political leader inspires the support of a wide-ranging coalition of interests that includes business, philanthropy, culture, economic development, entertainment, and other government entities. St. Paul's remarkable rebirth as a historic river city is an inspiring story filled with compelling personalities and plenty of drama.

Best of all, it is a story that is still evolving.

Perhaps Norm Coleman's best legacy of all to St. Paul is his prediction that "the best is yet to come."

•••

This book is the collaboration of a handful of very talented writers and editors. They include Mary Lahr Schier, Gene Rebeck, Suzy Frisch, Chris Mikko, Ingrid Case, Mike Finley, Andrew Bacskai, and Jacquelyn Fletcher.

I assigned chapters to be written individually, so that each writer would take a special ownership of his or her topic and ensure that it received an appropriate amount of attention. Too often, in a project like this, an individual writer will focus on the obvious "big picture" people and events and lose sight of the little details that are just as important.

I was careful to preserve the individual voice and perspective of each of the writers. Each chapter was written so that it would be enjoyed in sequence, but so that each could be read independently as well. I think the occasional repetitive information is worth the flexibility it brings on.

Thanks to everyone who was interviewed or otherwise contributed to this book. Norm Coleman not only endured more than a dozen individual interviews from writers, but also spent hours and hours with me, helping ensure we got it right. John Labosky, president and CEO of the Capital City Partnership, spent even more time with writers and me, as did Lee Koch, the Partnership's vice president and director of marketing. These two are special people, whose loyalty and selfless energies on behalf of St. Paul will continue long after Mayor Coleman has left office.

Extra special thanks goes to Chris Mikko, who was a colleague of mine at *Twin Cities Business Monthly* and who I persuaded to join Mason Smiley Larson, Ltd., just in time for him to take on a month's worth of 70-hour work-weeks as we got this little book ready for the printer. Without his whip-cracking sensibilities, this book might still be sitting at the bottom of my briefcase.

—Tom Mason

Building the Vision

After a visit to Minnesota's booming capital, Mark Twain wrote approvingly that "St. Paul is a city made out of brick and stone with an air of intending to stay."

But by the early 1990s, the durability of downtown St. Paul looked extremely doubtful. True, most downtowns throughout the United States have struggled in the postwar era. But St. Paul seemed to be hopelessly ensnared in a downward spiral. The city's commercial multi-tenant office vacancy rates were over 20 percent, and the vacancy rates in the retail sector were even higher. Several large businesses had left the city, and major hotels had shut their doors. The problems seemed insurmountable: To the rest of the city, downtown appeared to be a liability, not an asset.

This was the situation Norm Coleman faced when he became mayor in January 1994. In response, the new mayor had preached a message of hope. St. Paul's best days, he declared, were still ahead of it; the best was yet to come. But he knew he needed to build upon that vision, turning hope into confidence, and confidence into investment.

In short, he needed allies. So he reached out to members of the business community for resources and expertise. One of the first he called upon was Doug Leatherdale, CEO of The St. Paul

Companies. A long-time pillar in the community, Doug Leatherdale ran a company employing 3,000 in the downtown core, occupying more than 1 million square feet of office space, and bearing the city's name as its own. He would prove to be indispensable in helping the new mayor gather other business leaders in and around St. Paul into a public-private partnership.

In the summer of 1995, I got a call from Mayor Coleman asking for advice in developing this new partnership. I was then CEO of of the Minneapolis Downtown Council, an organization in many respects similar to the one the mayor was envisioning. The following January, my wife, Julie, and I had dinner with Mayor Coleman, and he asked whether I would take over the leadership of what would come to be called the Capital City Partnership.

From a personal standpoint, the job had numerous attractions. One was the opportunity to use all of my professional experience. Before joining the Downtown Council, I had served as CEO of Ellerbe Becket, one of the largest architectural firms in the nation, and my background encompassed architecture, engineering, and law. As head of the Council, I'd worked with many of the CEOs who the mayor had been reaching out to, and they encouraged me to join the efforts in St. Paul.

But above all, the appeal was the city itself. Downtown St. Paul is a unique urban environment. Like Rome, it is built upon seven hills. Upon one of the highest of these hills sits the great State Capitol, designed by Cass Gilbert, who also created the U.S. Capitol in Washington D.C. Also influencing the city's distinctive topography is the Mississippi River, with magnificent bluffs rising 90 feet from the banks—right in the heart of town. Though St. Paul's streets were largely laid out on a grid, the grid bends with the river, resulting in a number of irregular blocks, and buildings configured accordingly. For the visitor, particularly the pedestrian, this creates a constant sense of visual surprise.

In many respects, St. Paul is more of an Eastern city than a Western one. With its relatively short blocks, narrow streets, and geographic idiosyncrasies, it shares some of the urban intimacy found in cities like Boston and Providence. Historically, its buildings have reflected this, generally projecting a horizontal feeling, as opposed to the impersonal verticality of International Style glass blocks.

In short, as Mayor Coleman made clear, the city of St. Paul had a great deal going for it. In financial terms, St. Paul was like a stock at its 52-week low, but one with a lot of upside potential. The opportunity to work for such a city—and with a dynamic leader like the mayor—was too good to pass up.

The autumn before I came on board, Mayor Coleman and then-Governor Arne Carlson had assembled a group of business and government leaders to discuss the prospects of the state's capital city. The meeting's goal was to create a new, more hopeful vision for downtown St. Paul. Included in that group was Kenneth Greenberg, an urban planner from Toronto who would play a key behind-the-scenes role in St. Paul's future. In building this vision, the group was tackling one great, overarching question: How do you build a great city?

This book details our answer to that question. What we wished to create was a sustainable cycle of revitalizing the city and encouraging its future growth. These steps, which are both systematic and interrelated, are to (1) expand downtown employment by retaining and expanding the commercial office core; (2) increase the number of entertainment venues so that St. Paul would not be an 8-to-5 city; (3) broaden and promote the city's arts and culture offerings; (4) stimulate more residential development in the city center; and (5) promote the rebirth of downtown as a rich and varied retail environment.

While this five-step process is an ongoing one, it has already shown astonishing results. The word many people, both residents and outside observers, have used to describe the progress of downtown St. Paul over the past six years is "renaissance," and they point to such high-profile projects as the Xcel Energy Center, the Science Museum of Minnesota, Lawson Commons, and the return of major league hockey to St. Paul with the Minnesota

Wild. But behind the scenes, statistics bring additional dimensions to this remarkable story: 18,000 new jobs created, $3.5 billion in new construction ($1.7 billion of that in downtown), 1.75 million square feet of net office-space absorption, a per-annum average of 20 percent increases in the assessed value of downtown commercial property for five consecutive years. As a result of these efforts, Standard & Poor's gave the city a AAA bond rating in 2001—the first time in the city's history that this rating had been achieved.

But perhaps an even higher recognition of the city's turn-around occurred in January 2001, when the U.S. Conference of Mayors gave the Capital City Partnership its award of excellence for private-public partnerships. Rightfully, Mayor Coleman himself accepted this prestigious honor.

It is true that there is still much to do. The process of city-building never ends. It never should end. Yet it also is true that under Norm Coleman's leadership, downtown St. Paul has broken the spiral of hopelessness, replacing it with an ever-deepening sense of confidence. To use Mark Twain's words, St. Paul is once again a city intending to stay.

• • •

In building upon the mayor's vision, special mention should be made to the city leaders who believed in that vision, and who each played an essential, integral role in the city's achievement. These individuals are the members of the Development Cabinet, a group assembled and led by Mayor Coleman to unify and prioritize its city-building efforts. The cabinet's success has been due to the mayor's leadership and the mutual affection and respect that developed among its members.

Susan Kimberly serves as deputy mayor and chief of staff for the Mayor's Office. Susan brings a wealth of knowledge and history of St. Paul to the process, and has been a steadying influence, always looking to advance the action.

Brian Sweeney, who has headed up the city's Department of Planning & Economic Development since March 1999, is a savvy leader who possesses a personal style that wears well with everyone around him. One inevitable characteristic of any development project is that it will fall apart at least two or three times before it finally comes together. Brian's disarming sense of humor has helped us temper the ups and persevere through the downs without losing focus.

Ken Johnson, the president and CEO of the St. Paul Port Authority—in essence, the city's industrial development champion—has deep roots in St. Paul's economic development world, which have given him a wide net of personal contacts and institutional knowledge, in addition to an unparalleled know-how in public finance.

Vic Wittgenstein worked his way through every job there is at Parks & Recreation before becoming its director. As someone who is completely devoted and dedicated to St. Paul's parks, he understands how they are an amenity that enhances St. Paul's broader quality of life.

Tom Eggum, who heads the city's Department of Public Works, has never said, "it can't be done." As a civil engineer, he has always been willing to roll up his sleeves and figure out how to solve a problem, and always within the realities of budget limits and the context of ongoing projects.

As head of the St. Paul Riverfront Corp., which is funded primarily by the McKnight and St. Paul Foundations, Patrick Seeb has provided a point of view from the philanthropic and charitable-foundation world. His love of the Mississippi River—its history, its neighborhoods, and its potential as a focus for city-building—has been an engine of success for numerous projects.

Erich Mische has been a valued member of Mayor Coleman's team, and has worked in a variety of capacities for the City of St. Paul over the years, bringing energy, enthusiasm, and keen insight to each one.

John Gutzmann, director of the city's Department of Public

Housing, retains a big-picture orientation while never losing sight of his mission to provide quality affordable housing for the people of St. Paul.

Among the scores of others who deserve mention, space requirements limit me to just three more.

I mentioned Doug Leatherdale earlier, but I'd like to add more here. The first chairman of the Capital City Partnership, he has been a great mentor and a great supporter of St. Paul. Many of the accomplishments listed in this book would not have happened without his leadership and activism.

Al Schuman, president and CEO of Ecolab, is the Partnership's current chair and has done a superb job picking up where Doug Leatherdale left off. Al has been a steadfast activist with a focus on revitalizing St. Paul's downtown core. Ecolab Plaza, which fronts his company's headquarters on Wabasha Street, has become one of the focal points of the downtown revival.

Robert Senkler, president and CEO of Minnesota Life, is succeeding Al Schuman as the Partnership's chair. With Norm Coleman ending his tenure as mayor in January 2001, Bob will play a key role in meeting the challenge of guiding St. Paul through the post-Coleman era. He brings to the job a strong sense that we need to redouble our efforts in the neighborhoods, because the destinies of the neighborhoods and the downtown core are so profoundly entwined. Still in his 40s, he represents the next generation of St. Paul's leadership.

It has been a great privilege for me to work with all of these people. If you seek their monuments, visit downtown St. Paul—and look at what surrounds you.

John Labosky
President and CEO
Capital City Partnership
St. Paul, Minnesota
November 7, 2001

CEOs: Norm Coleman's Executive Operation

St. Paul found a powerful new ally
in the form of a long-neglected resource:
the local business community.

BY MARY LAHR SCHIER

Martin Luther King Day, 1996. Outside the St. Paul Hotel, a cold January snow falls lightly. Inside the basement dining room, a blizzard of conversation swirls. Look one direction, you'll see Bob Ulrich, head of the Dayton's and Target stores. Look another and find Jim Howard, NSP's CEO. Dick Kovacevich has driven over from the Minneapolis headquarters of Norwest Banks, and Michael Bonsignore of Honeywell is there too. The room is packed, wall-to-wall power, probably more expensive dark gray suits in one place than St. Paul has seen in a decade. Mayor Norm Coleman works the room. They are all there to talk about the future of St. Paul, not only about giving advice, but in how they each could invest their time and money into turning the city around. This meeting represents a triumph for Coleman, the culmination of two years of speech-making, strategizing, and politicking. He's finally got the members of the business community interested in St. Paul—now what's he going to do with them?

The genesis of the meeting occurred two years earlier and two blocks away, in an upper-story office of The St. Paul Companies. Coleman had just been elected mayor. In early 1994, he went to visit Douglas Leatherdale, CEO of The St. Paul Companies, downtown St. Paul's largest employer and owner of about a million square feet of prime downtown real estate. Unlike other CEOs around town who had backed the young attorney in his run for mayor, Leatherdale hadn't endorsed Coleman or given him campaign money. Still, Leatherdale liked that Coleman had asked to meet him, the first mayor of St. Paul to do so. The two hit it off immediately and Leatherdale spoke frankly.

"It's obvious to both you and me that this city needs a lot of help," Leatherdale recalls telling the mayor. "I suggested to him that one of the things Minneapolis had that St. Paul did not—one of the things that made it vibrant—was the Minneapolis Club. Business people belong to the club. They support the club. You could go in there any day of the week for lunch and get a lot of business done. You could see everybody who really mattered there."

St. Paul had no such gathering space for executives, and some wondered if the city had any significant business leadership at all. Downtown real estate had been losing value since the 1980s and the skyways looked deserted, except for discount stores and delis. In 1985, the Project for Corporate Responsibility studied the influence business had on civic affairs in the Twin Cities. The study found an influential pocket in downtown Minneapolis and one centered on the Minnesota Business Partnership, but visible business leadership had faded completely in St. Paul.

St. Paul desperately needed such leadership. In the early 1990s, St. Paul was "tired and bleak," according to Howard, who retired as CEO and chairman of Xcel Energy (formerly NSP) in 2001. Howard understood the difference business leaders could make in the future of a city. He grew up in Pittsburgh, right after World

War II. Smoke hung over Pittsburgh then, a reminder of its industrial past. The city glowed orange at night as moonlight and lamplight filtered through the haze. Polluted and ugly, despite the natural beauty of the Allegheny Valley in which it sat, Pittsburgh slid into economic and social decline in the early 20th century—and stayed there. The city deserved its reputation as "Hell with the lid taken off."

Then, as Howard tells it, two people got together. Pittsburgh Mayor David L. Lawrence was a Roman Catholic, a Democrat, the son of a laborer. He worked his way into the mayor's office in 1945 via machine politics and a penchant for campaigning 15 hours a day. In 1946, the gregarious Lawrence met Richard King Mellon, a quiet billionaire with more interest in hunting moose than running a business. But Mellon loved Pittsburgh, the town in which his family made its fortune, and he took its decline personally. The two men forged an unlikely alliance. They convinced the railroads to stop running coal trains through the city. They convinced foundries to install smoke-control devices. With Lawrence's political drive and Mellon's contacts among business and social leaders, the Allegheny Conference for Community Development began to rebuild Pittsburgh.

"Essentially, they saved the city," recalls Howard, from his home in Florida. "What I saw as a young guy was what could happen when people from business and people from politics got together."

St. Paul in 1993 did not look like hell with the lid off—too dull for that. But the city was worn down and depressed In 1992, West Publishing, after 114 years anchoring downtown St. Paul's western border, moved to Eagan, pulling more than 2,000 workers out of downtown. Later that year, First Bank System moved 720 downtown employees to Energy Park. The downtown Holiday Inn closed. Condominiums in downtown buildings sold for half what they had been priced at 10 years earlier. Office vacancy rates—high all over the Twin Cities—were highest in St. Paul, where they hung around 20 percent. The property values of downtown businesses also had declined, dropping an average of 46 percent between 1988 and 1994. Storefronts, both on the street and in the skyways, sat empty. Moreover, downtown died at 5 p.m. and everyone knew it. The city had only one really good restaurant and the only signs of life at night shuttled between the Ordway Theater and the Saint Paul Hotel.

"St. Paul's main problem was low self-esteem," says urban planner Ken Greenberg of Greenberg Consultants Ltd., a Toronto-based architectural firm, who helped the city design a framework for river development.

Peter Ridder came to St. Paul in 1992 to work as publisher of the *St. Paul Pioneer Press*. He immediately sensed the city's funk. "St. Paul had no real direction, no political direction," says Ridder, now publisher of the *Charlotte Observer*. "Don't get me wrong. [Former mayor] Jim Scheibel is a great humanist, but his interests were not in business or economic development. He really did not see that there was no vitality, that there was no optimism in the community."

The business community had lost touch with government. They felt that the politicos who ran St. Paul viewed business, especially big business, as a necessary evil. Talk swirled among corporate suites about the time The St. Paul Companies hosted a grand-opening party to celebrate its purchase of the long-ailing historic St. Paul Hotel. Missing from the impressive groups of business and political dignitaries was Mayor Jim Scheibel. He was across the street in Rice Park, protesting homelessness by spending the night sleeping in a cardboard box.

"We lost the corporate leaders in this community for awhile," says Tom Kingston, president of the Amherst Wilder Foundation, a social service provider in St. Paul. "Every company is international. They are so pressured by Wall Street. What died was the CEOs coming together to talk about anything in the community and trying to find ways to help."

"People could see what was happening in St. Paul and they talked about it, but there was never a political guy who really wanted to do anything about it," says Howard. "Norm Coleman called on the business community and said, 'We are going to get something going.' All he really did was ask."

Outreach

Norm Coleman had been courting the business community since his campaign began in early 1993. As one of 16 candidates for mayor, he distinguished himself by promoting economic development, especially along the riverfront, as his top campaign promise. Business leaders, glad to see someone with an appreciation for business running for office, moved into the Coleman camp. "He was a moderate," says Pierson "Sandy" Grieve, CEO of Ecolab Inc. until 1995, and an early Coleman supporter. "Frankly, at the time there was a lack of support from the city. They did not give a damn about whether downtown businesses were growing or not."

CEOs immediately sensed Coleman's sincere interest in business. "I got very tight with him," says Al Schuman, who succeeded Grieve at Ecolab. "He was a guy who said something and then did it. When you're a CEO, you have to be a leader. You have to take control to grow a company. It's the same with a city. We knew Coleman could take control."

Coleman's early days in office impressed business leaders as much as his promises. On his second day as mayor, Coleman met with a large group of business owners to outline a plan to reinvest in downtown and the river. He set up one-on-one meetings with CEOs to get their ideas for St. Paul. Coleman's staff appointments included people business owners respected, such as Larry Buegler, the former president of Norwest Bank-St. Paul, named the new director of the city's Planning & Economic Development department, and Dick Broeker, who spent 10 years doing economic development for former Mayor George Latimer, as director of the St. Paul Riverfront Corp.

Coleman also kept his promises to hold the line on city spending. Three months into 1994, he challenged a contract with one of the city's powerful employee unions—a contract that would have cost the city millions in health care expenses. Six months later, he cut 20 staff positions in Planning & Economic Development because of cost overruns. Wherever he went—and he seemed to be everywhere—Coleman described an economically vibrant St. Paul, with a lively downtown core connected to its roots at the Mississippi River. While some admired Coleman's vision of a glorious river city, others thought he was promoting a fantasy.

At one meeting, downtown building owners practically hooted the new mayor. "There was just a lot of heavy, heavy negativity," recalls Broeker, "A lot of complaining and carping, a lot of old wounds people wanted to talk about. It was particularly rough when he was pitching riverfront development. People did not want to hear that. They said, 'We're bleeding in downtown and you want to talk about the river?!'"

"I don't think anyone who came out of St. Paul's traditional business or political establishment could have helped us break out of that mindset," says Tim Marx, an attorney with Briggs and Morgan.

So Coleman found friends among the business community, especially Leatherdale. "Leatherdale understood the need to create a big vision," says Pat Seeb, executive director of the St. Paul Riverfront Corp. "It was natural for him to see the visionary quality of what the city was planning to do. And there was good chemistry with Coleman. They liked each other."

Adds Broeker: "Leatherdale's a tough guy. He knows a good thing when he sees it."

Coleman had studied the business leaders and quickly concluded that the real value was in personal relationships. As Coleman methodically met with every business leader who would see him, either personally or in groups, he was stunned to see the isolation with which St. Paul had run business. "Norm understood the importance of personal relationships," says Don Garofalo, president and CEO of Andersen Corp. in Bayport. "Here was a man who was busy with so many things, but he always remembered the big things and the little things. He paid everyone a tremendous amount of respect. He even came to my son's funeral."

"Jim Scheibel never broke bread with these folks," Coleman says. "Of course they didn't feel included."

Coleman took it further. He sought out mentor relationships, he asked business leaders about how to manage huge organizations, how he could bring efficiency and effectiveness to government in the same way they got it from business. "I'm not sure anyone had ever asked them for advice before," Coleman remembers. "They were eager to help. They all told me the same thing, although sometimes in different ways: They talked about having a core vision, of knowing where you want to go and what you want to accomplish. They talked a lot about focus, about motivating people, and getting their focus."

The conversations reinforced Coleman's focus on the river. He attracted political support too, most importantly from Governor Arne Carlson. "When I started to hear Coleman talk about the river, I called him up," Carlson says. "And remember, he was still a Democrat, so some people in my party weren't crazy about me working with him. But I called him up and said, 'From here on out we're partners.'"

"What became clear as we started the riverfront initiatives was that we had lots of philanthropic support and the mayor could provide city support," says Seeb. "The missing ingredient was corporate interest."

To build that interest, Coleman first forged alliances with CEOs who had a personal stake in downtown St. Paul, big employers like Ecolab and Minnesota Mutual. It was a natural match. Ecolab, for example, almost left St. Paul in the mid-1990s, but stayed in part because leaders sensed the town was about to turn around. It was what one observer called "a leap of faith."

"Taxes here are not God's gift to humanity, and neither is the weather," says CEO Schuman. "I told Norm about [leaving] and frankly, he's a great salesman. I felt a loyalty to employees, but we had chances to be in places like Florida or Texas where they don't have taxes like we have here and they don't have the weather. We would have lost some employees, but a lot of them would have come with us. I spoke to Coleman and he said, 'These are the kind of things I'm planning to do,' and I said, 'OK, I'll help you.'"

Says Leatherdale: "I had very selfish motivations for getting involved. I had a very major stake in this city, both in terms of employees and shareholders."

In 1995, Coleman expanded the group through a series of breakfasts at which he could explain his hopes for St. Paul to business leaders. The presentations always included the display of a drawing done by St. Paul native and architect Benjamin Thompson of how the Mississippi River could look, if the city developed it as a park. The city owned several versions of Thompson's image—spring, summer, fall—and all of them showed a lush, human-scale riverscape nestled against a warm and thriving downtown. "That drawing was pure poetry—nothing like the way the river really looked," says Broeker. "But we took it everywhere we went."

"At these meetings, they talked a lot about what makes a city great," says Capital City Partnership President and CEO John Labosky, who sat in on some meetings in his former capacity as president of the Minneapolis Downtown Council. "Executives travel a lot. They talked about places like London and Paris and New York and what makes them great. It was the mixed uses that made a city great. It was the density that made a city great. You cannot be just a commercial center and be a great city. You can't have people work there but not live there. You have to have people come at night and on weekends for entertainment. They should come for the arts and the cultural events. We have a lot of things in St. Paul that the suburbs don't."

The drawing, the dismal conditions the city faced, and Coleman's relentless salesmanship brought more CEOs to the table. Ridder got more involved and his newspaper ran a series of editorials about riverfront development. Howard and Ulrich started to see the possibilities in St. Paul. The St. Paul CEOs also found support from media owners, like Stanley Hubbard of KSTP-TV and *Minneapolis Star Tribune* publisher Jay Cowles. Financiers like Addison Piper of Piper Jaffray and John Grundhofer of First Bank System also expressed interest. "I knew from the day I met him that this was a guy I could support," says Garofalo. "Norm's a holistic thinker. He sees the big picture—and he sees how all the pieces fit together within that picture. He brought everybody together, he was kind of like a master architect."

At one meeting, Ulrich rhapsodized about Quebec City, a town in which he'd vacationed several times. Ulrich grew up in St. Paul and played football at Central High School. He had a fondness for his hometown and says he saw something of it in Quebec City. The St. Lawrence River winds through Quebec City, just as the Mississippi curves around downtown St. Paul, and the Chateau Frantenac looks down on the town from above and away just as the Capitol seems to gaze toward downtown St. Paul and the river. "I remember hearing Ulrich describe Quebec City that way and a light bulb just went off in my head. I thought, 'Hey, he's not too far off,'" says Broeker.

As meetings among CEOs and Coleman staff continued, both sides realized this could be a significant partnership. The CEOs could think big and dream for the city. They were unencumbered by political considerations or an opposition party, and gave Coleman a way to avoid those forces. CEOs did not have to run through all the approvals or regulations every city project might require if the city did it alone. They also had access to money, especially as Minnesota's economy went into overdrive about 1995.

"If you get to the CEO, things can happen very quickly and outside the box," says Marx, who served as deputy mayor in the mid-1990s. "There was a perceived and actual need to have a specific mechanism for CEOs to take a vested interest in St. Paul. CEOs are a different breed and they need to be engaged differently. We had to find ways to engage them on terms on which they were willing to be engaged."

CEOs "can get together and have a lot of good ideas, but then we go back to our desks," says Robert Senkler, CEO of Minnesota Life. "We needed an organization like the Capital City Partnership to harness those ideas."

Coleman and Leatherdale had already been thinking about who might lead this new organization. They wanted a person who understood what it meant to run a company and who also understood the public sector. They immediately settled on Labosky. CEOs who had been part of some of Coleman's early meetings served on the board of Labosky's current employer, the Minneapolis Downtown Council. Labosky had previously been CEO of the architectural, engineering, and planning firm of Ellerbe Becket. He had every quality Leatherdale and Coleman were seeking.

Peter Ridder was with Coleman and Leatherdale in the summer of 1995 when they met with Labosky in the bar of the St. Paul Hotel to talk about the possibility of Labosky moving over from Minneapolis. "We got lucky," says Ridder. "John had wanted a new challenge and felt St. Paul was certainly that."

"Some of the CEOs who approached me had been on my board in Minneapolis," says Labosky. "So I had my own board coming and saying, 'How would you like to revitalize the other Twin City?'"

That fall, Governor Carlson hosted a breakfast meeting at the Governor's Residence to make a more formal pitch for the new CEO organization. "We really worked those phones," says Broeker. "We invited everybody from Cargill in Minnetonka to Andersen Windows in Stillwater. But we had a restriction. We said, 'We want the CEO to come. If you can't make it, don't bother to send anyone else.' We wanted this to be an organization for CEOs."

Of the 24 invited CEOs, 16 attended. Greenberg described how the riverfront could be developed. Coleman spoke about projects he hoped to bring to fruition in St. Paul: a new Science Museum, a remodeled convention center, a hockey arena, more commercial spaces and housing. "It was a good show, but we had some credible people behind us," says Broeker. The meeting created enough enthusiasm that the leadership group decided to make a formal pitch. They invited an even larger group of CEOs to lunch at the Saint Paul Hotel. They decided a few things about how this organization would work from the beginning. First, it would be a CEO organization; personal involvement was the key to getting things done. CEOs who had worked with Coleman knew they could expect a call from him a few times a month—either to ask for help or to offer assistance. It would be these personal relationships that moved projects forward.

"Without the personal involvement of CEOs we wouldn't accomplish the things we needed," Coleman says, adding, however, that it was about more than their ability to commit resources. "In many ways they are more 'can do' than the people around them. They have ingenuity and creativity. And they are not afraid to take risks in pursuit of an overall vision."

Second, the focus would be on redeveloping downtown with a preference for projects that would create visibility and pull people into the city core. Finally, the group would work for the Capital City Partnership—not St. Paul—and it would include CEOs from companies from the western edge of the Twin Cities to the Wisconsin border. "This wouldn't have worked without the focus on the capital city," says Leatherdale, who lives in western Hennepin County and works for several Minneapolis-based charities, including the Minnesota Orchestra. "It had to be the whole Twin Cities, not just St. Paul. If we had not done that we would have had all the old, archaic Minneapolis-vs.-St. Paul arguments. That was the hook. People come from all over the world to visit here. Did we want them to see a rundown capital city?"

"We're really one city," says Schuman, a native New Yorker who speaks in a rapid-fire manner. "Forget the politics that are here. Are downtown and uptown Manhattan different cities? We're all New Yorkers. In any normal area, you'd have one city. What's good for St. Paul is good for Minneapolis and vice versa."

"I told the CEOs that I needed two things," says Labosky. "First, they needed to fund the organization—$25,000 a year per company—so I would not have to spend all my time raising money. Second, and most important, I insisted on an active board."

"When the mayor spoke, he said, 'I'm willing to do my part—provide the organization, the staff, reduce crime, clean the street, but I need each of you too,'" Seeb recalls. "It was evident St. Paul was at a crossroads. The mayor and the Partnership gave the CEOs a conduit to make a difference."

By the time the lunch was over, the nucleus of a partnership existed, and "since I called the meeting and paid for lunch, I ended up being chair," jokes Leatherdale. In April 1996, CEOs from 20 Twin Cities companies announced the formation of the Capital City Partnership, a group to plan, develop, promote, and market downtown St. Paul and to encourage economic development in the city.

Jumpstart

Once formed, the Partnership leaders wanted to make an immediate impact on the city. By 1996, the economy had improved considerably and the time was ripe to jumpstart St. Paul's economy. The Partnership quickly bought the Taste of Minnesota, which was then $200,000 in debt, because Labosky believed the festival could be a moneymaker for the Partnership. With Carlson's unwavering support, $30 million in state bonding passed for the Science Museum of Minnesota, guaranteeing a new jewel on the river for the city. In 1997, plans were announced for a new, $54 million office tower in the block between Wabasha and St. Peter Streets and Fifth and Sixth to house Lawson Software, the first large employer to move into downtown in years.

"It was important to have a couple of visible wins," says Senkler. Those victories, and the renewed confidence the city exuded, were among the reasons Senkler's company decided in 1997 to build a second office tower along Robert Street.

The Capital City Partnership provided a forum for executives to talk about what the city needed and a direction for corporate giving. The personal involvement of executives and their companies has been a key to the Partnership's success, says Labosky. When the financing to build the Lawson Commons looked like it might not work, it came together in part because Doug Leatherdale's St. Paul Companies was willing to lease more than 30 percent of the office space in the building.

The Partnership stepped in again on the second half of that project, when plans were made for a $16 million, city-owned parking ramp behind the Lawson building. The city had money for the ramp, but nothing more. Labosky and the city wanted to use the ramp to encourage more activity along the street. "We went back to the business community to ask for help to make the ramp look like a streetscape and actually build retail spaces into the street level," says Labosky. Companies contributed millions to fund the retail spaces around the tower, which now features an eyeglass shop, bustling coffee shops, and restaurants.

When the NHL was considering locating its expansion team in St. Paul, the league expressed concern that there would not be enough corporate support for the team. In short, it wanted assurances that it would have income from luxury boxes, sponsorships, and naming rights on the new hockey arena. "I got on the phone and by the end of the day I had 50 letters faxed to me pledging to buy luxury suites," says Labosky. "Seven wanted larger sponsorships and three were interested in naming rights on the arena."

Similarly, members of the Partnership paid $4,100 each to buy Snoopy statues that could be displayed in public spaces around St. Paul during the year 2000. The companies then gave the statues back to the Partnership, which sold them at an auction to raise funds to install bronze versions of the "Peanuts Gang" statues in a downtown park. Partnership firms also helped raise $50,000 a year for three years to run the Capital City Trolley before it could grow into a profitable private service.

CEOs have been eager to be involved, and not always for civic reasons alone. Having a vibrant downtown makes it easier for companies to recruit and retain workers, an issue many Twin Cities firms struggled with during the late 1990s. Says Schuman: "What [a strong downtown] means is that you can attract people to the city now. If I cannot go out and recruit the smartest people, how am I going to grow my business? Why would someone from Stanford or Harvard or Northwestern want to come here? This place was Deadsville for a long time. Now we've given them a reason to come."

Schuman recalls that when he moved to St. Paul after 15 years commuting from New York City, some of his staff suggested he take an apartment downtown to be closer to work. "I said, 'Are you kidding? What am I going to do at night?' I'd be divorced if I'd done that," he says. The Capital City Partnership has made a difference, one that its CEO leaders can see and feel.

On a summer Friday night in 2001, Schuman walked around a downtown completely different from the one he would not live in a few years earlier. A crowd was gathering outside the Ordway. An antique car show was being held on the other end of the city. Tourists stopped to take pictures of their kids in the arms of a Charlie Brown statue. The Minnesota Orchestra was tuning up for a performance on Harriet Island. "The city was jumping, just jumping," says Schuman. "There was a nice European flair to it. You add more of these things to downtown and you've got life."

That life will not fade when Coleman leaves office, Partnership leaders say. "Coleman was the catalyst, the guy who put the vision out," says Schuman. "But right now we have a very strong organization. I think of the Capital City Partnership as a second line of defense against mediocrity. We will have the flowers in the streets whether Coleman is there or not. We will have the Snoopys and the Charlie Browns. I tell all our members the job in St. Paul is not done. Norm set us off, but there's a lot left to do. We've still got housing to do; we've still got to work on retail."

Adds Senkler: "Clearly, our challenge is to prove that we have built something of value. If we cannot keep this going because we have lost one leader, then we haven't created anything of value. I see it as the difference between a good company and a great one. With a good company, a CEO can come in, get people fired up, and turn it around. But when he leaves, the company flounders. A great company can go from one leader to the next without losing momentum. We need to prove that St. Paul is a great city in that way.

"The leadership might be more or less than we've had in the past; the economy might be better or worse than we've had in the past," he adds. "The proof that we have a great city will be if we don't miss Coleman when he leaves. That would be his greatest legacy."

River of Dreams

The Mississippi is at the heart of a reborn St. Paul.

BY MICHAEL FINLEY

"If I look to the future of a signature of a Coleman administration, I hope that riverfront development will be something that will stand out. It is one of our tremendous natural resources that should draw people here."
—*Mayor Norm Coleman speech, January 1994*

A reporter once asked a key question of Dick Broeker, a retired consultant who played a key role developing the St. Paul riverfront: "What was the moment you realized the city was about to undergo a fantastic transformation?"

Broeker frowned and replied: "It was in a meeting with Norm Coleman, the new mayor. It was in April of 1994. I knew Coleman a bit. I have to tell you I did not vote for the guy. He was the sort of person you sometimes meet who's so ambitious, who has such big ideas, you wonder if he's completely for real.

"It was over lunch at Tommy J's, on Selby Avenue, and Norm was sick. I mean, he had the flu and he did not look good. Up until this time, he had tried to get me interested in rebuilding St. Paul, because I was involved in riverfront redevelopment work with Mayor Latimer in the 1980s. But now I was retired. I didn't have the stomach for some enormous new project. Not from some politician with a head full of ideas.

"But he had the flu, and he looked like hell, and it was late, but he kept going on about what could happen if people could just see what he saw. Because it was all doable. And it was then that a little light went on in me. I was no longer listening because he was the mayor, or to humor him; he had gotten to me.

"You see, it occurred to me that only a certain kind of guy is going to be talking up the city when he feels that bad. And I thought, 'I want some of what he's having.' So I went home that night and told my wife I kind of liked the new mayor after all.

"Monday morning, I called him back and gave him my answer. "'OK, Norm. Let's get to work.'"

A city on the Father of Waters

"The Mississippi. At the heart of the city. The very essence of our beginning as a community. It will be a squandered resource no more."
—*Mayor Coleman, State of the City Address, March 1994*

"Find the water, and you'll find the people." The City of St. Paul, Minnesota spent over a century violating that adage. For many years it turned its back on the river that was its very reason for existing. But today, thanks to a major refocusing effort by the city, we're seeing the river again, and we're liking what we see.

The Mississippi was what brought early settlers to St. Paul: it provided food, water, a way to move about, and the tactical leverage of being at the topmost navigable point on North America's biggest river. It was a place to live; early residents built their homes and businesses along the river. The Mississippi was where things happened. The Minnesota men who fought for the Union in the Civil War left to great fanfare via the Mississippi; at Gettysburg, seven of every eight would die. Earlier, in 1854, a group of journalists joined then-President Millard Fillmore in a trip upriver from Rock Island, Ill., to St. Paul. This trip was a national news event of the day, spawning stories in virtually every major American newspaper.

The river was everything—sustenance, transportation, a way to conduct commerce, and a place to look down on from high up. In the 19th century people knew what they had. The original plans of architect Cass Gilbert, who designed the state capitol building and the great lawn laid out below it, called for a much bigger mall, one extending all the way down to the water, just as the Great Mall in Washington dips a toe in the Potomac. Land speculators prevented that dream from taking hold, however.

In the early part of the 20th century, however, all that changed. The land along the riverfront became increasingly industrialized. Manufacturing and storage sites became a kind of dirty curtain, separating the city from the river. Industrial sights, sounds, and smells made the Mississippi less than appealing.

Unsavory detail: The city's human wastes were routinely dumped in the Mississippi, along with its industrial wastes, creating a pungent olfactory stew. At one point, a group of engineers were called to investigate a new island that had surfaced in the Mississippi. Their discovery? The island was not composed of dirt.

The decline in quality during the first decades of this century was precipitous. The number and varieties of life in and around the river plummeted. Where once more than 30 species of fish thrived, all disappeared except three. Eagles died out, as the river's DDT pesticide levels made their eggshells in bluff nests too fragile for chicks to survive. Mayflies—one of the humbler mainstays of the regional food chain—nearly died out. Likewise, human beings began to shun the river. Where once as many as 20,000 weekend visitors had once picnicked and boated, by the 1920s not even the fish and the birds could be persuaded to stay.

Even when industry began to move out of the riverfront area, the land and water remained polluted by industrial and human waste. The situation began to improve in the 1930s, when the Pig's Eye sewage treatment plant was constructed. Pig's Eye helped clean up human waste in the river, though industrial dumping still occurred. In the early 1970s, new rules requiring that sanitary sewers had to be separate from waste helped improve the river's demeanor, as did improvements to the city's storm sewer system. After banning DDT, eagles began returning to nesting sites along the river bluffs.

Beginning in the 1960s, a series of St. Paul city administrations, including that of former mayor George Latimer in the 1980s, took steps to clean up the river. Dick Broeker, Latimer's deputy mayor, and the brain behind much of the city's Lowertown redevelopment, was one of the first to fall under the river's spell. Where other people saw junk and deterioration, Broeker saw possibilities. But there was no leverage at that moment, either political or economic, for effecting grand change. "There was just no heart for it," Broeker says, "no spirit for it." To get things going, he says, you need someone with a big horn and good lungs. No administration was able to make improvement of the Mississippi riverfront a top priority. Until 1994.

Coleman's bluff

"And cities, like people, need hope to grow and prosper. I believe we can find renewed hope by tapping into the rich resources of the Mississippi River—and when I talk about riverfront redevelopment it's more than a project or a bridge—it's you and me, our parents, our children coming together sharing the richness of our history and uniting in the possibility of our future."
—Mayor Norm Coleman, State of the City Address, February 1995

The year 1993 saw the election of St. Paul Mayor Norm Coleman, a son of New York City whose local credentials included stints as chief prosecutor and solicitor general for the State of Minnesota. Fresh from victory, Coleman took a long look at the city he had to lead and sized up his situation. Though it had experienced some revival during the Latimer years, St. Paul was a city down on its heels.

Once the finer of the two Twin Cities, it now suffered from a sense of being the weak sister to sleek, economically with-it Minneapolis. Conspicuous corporate citizens were bolting their doors or stealing out of town. West Publishing, a major employer, had moved to the suburbs, leaving its giant riverside office building empty. The downtown Holiday Inn had closed, along with the St. Paul Athletic Club, and numerous other businesses. Downtown contained less than $300 million in taxable property, down from around $680 million a few short years earlier, in 1988. "People didn't have any confidence in the city or in the community itself," says Patrick Seeb, a one-time top aide to Coleman who later became executive director of the St. Paul Riverfront Corp. "There was a lot of skepticism."

Coleman sensed that the city needed a focus point for its revival. But what—a skyscraper, a sports stadium, another museum? Or something even bigger? "I was looking for some kind of symbolic linkage, something to rally around, something that was real, and that people would identify with," he says. He traveled to Harvard to learn about urban design. He called on former mayoral opponent Ray Faricy to head a study commission to explore opportunities for revitalizing the Mississippi. He traveled to other cities, as far away as San Antonio and Cleveland, and as nearby as Red Wing and Winona, gaining inspiration and a sense of opportunity, enabling him to think of the Mississippi River as the touchstone for a rebirth in St. Paul.

The irony was rich. The much-maligned river—never further, they say, than three miles from any point in the city—would draw the city together again, linking neighborhoods to downtown, and becoming the supple spine of a revivified St. Paul.

The notion was not greeted with enthusiasm in every corner. Seeb recalls a private meeting hosted by Peter Ridder, then publisher of the *St. Paul Pioneer Press*: "Peter wanted to bring together this young, energetic new mayor and downtown business leaders and property owners." Their response to Coleman's vision for riverfront development, according to Seeb "wasn't polite reluctance—it was downright opposition." Their concern, Coleman says, was that "We're dying, and here you're talking about a river four blocks away. You need to focus on the core downtown."

Broeker remembers how tough a sell it was. "You couldn't believe the beating Coleman took the first year. Everyone called him this mindless cheerleader who kept saying that St. Paul's best days are yet to come. We'd tell people at meeting after meeting that it was okay to be skeptical, but the question remained: 'Do you want St. Paul to thrive as a waterfront downtown or not?' And people would say, 'Well of course we want it to thrive, but that's never going to happen.' That was the standard response."

Not everyone, of course. Here and there a few civic leaders stepped up and acknowledged that the brash young mayor was onto something, and the city would be foolish not to hear him out. "Paul Verret was one, and Mike O'Keefe was another, and Doug Leatherdale of The St. Paul Companies stood up for the idea," Broeker says. "Bill Morrish from the University of Minnesota's Design Center was there, and a couple dozen other people who said, 'Hey, this is powerful stuff, let's put it into play, let's see if we can't get it moving forward.' Ron Clark of the *Pioneer Press* editorial page took us seriously from the first. Governor Arne Carlson soon became interested."

One person, then a dozen more, then a hundred, then an entire city—it was a classic story of communicating a vision and propagating it until it was irresistible.

One by one, Coleman and his supporters took business owners aside and explained how riverfront development could form part of a total plan for downtown economic revitalization, and how that phenomenon could then spread throughout the entire city. "We're treating downtown as the waterfront and the waterfront as downtown, which is the way St. Paul really grew up," Broeker says. People who had drifted away from the river lost their ability to see that connection. Coleman's task was to remind people of what once was, and what could be again. It was a bluff, in a sense, selling something marvelous that was as yet invisible. But Coleman saw it, and so he sold it, and sold it again.

Knowing the city hall would have a tough time effecting change on its own, Coleman revived and regrouped the St. Paul Riverfront Corp. He called on business and neighborhood leaders, civic activists, foundations, and public officials. Early supporters included Carl Drake, David Lilly, and Jay Cowles. And financial support soon flowed from the McKnight, F. R. Bigelow, and St. Paul Foundations.

Reconstructing the backbone

"Let's turn vision into action. I want you to join me as we initiate a reforestation project. By this fall we will plant over 12,000 trees, shrubs, and perennials."
—Mayor Coleman, State of the City Address, March 1994

Inspired by the vision of St. Paul native son and internationally recognized urban designer Ben Thompson, Coleman championed the idea of restoring the urban greenery. Thompson's concept of the Great River Park was his way of saying "if you should approach the entire river valley as a 'river park' and build out from that framework, you can't go wrong," according to Gregory K. Page, director of special projects at the St. Paul Riverfront Corp., and the group's unofficial historian.

So long as St. Paul remained a stewpot of industrial pollution, however, progress was impossible. Whole sections of riverfront property were occupied by industrial businesses. Some were past their prime and a few were downright unsightly. These properties were owned by a hodgepodge of businesses and individuals, who would have to be dealt with individually. Other sections were just blank spots, empty lots strewn with rubbish. The entire area was overrun with non-native vegetation—weeds.

The challenges involved in changing the area from a trashed waterfront to the centerpiece of a new St. Paul can hardly be underestimated. Private owners had to be contacted and negotiated with. The land had to be cleaned up, and where necessary, bull-dozed and recontoured. Then it had to be refurbished, with native plant species that could survive not just the Minnesota winter, but the havoc of living in a popular place. Last but not least was the problem of who would do the actual physical labor of installing and caring for new plantings.

To begin, Coleman put out a call to volunteers to go down to the river and collect the readily accessible junk for disposal. People did not respond all at once: some of the first trees were planted, not all that enthusiastically or well, by prisoners at Ramsey County Jail. Before long, however, regular citizens got word that something major was up, and then they responded, with greater enthusiasm than the people in lock-up. Almost immediately the riverfront looked better, minus its usual blanket of flotsam and debris.

With funding from The St. Paul Foundation, Coleman charged Great River Greening, a newly created organization, with the responsibility of replanting the riverfront area. When Great River Greening started excavating potential reforestation sites, they found asphalt, old roads, and brick from decayed buildings—but very little soil. What's more, they discovered that the soil pH of the land around the river was as high as the river itself —the result of limestone and cement particles.

And most of the land to be replanted was privately owned; some private landowners had to be convinced to accept and maintain public plantings on their land. Many of the landowners are small business owners working hard to survive, and they were not interested in any project that would cost them a lot of time and effort. The simple challenge of 'planting trees' was much more complicated than most realized.

Rob Buffler, the organization's executive director, brought in some secret weapons to get the job done: environmental experts and a local hockey star. While the need for environmental folks was apparent, Buffler also needed an ambassador. He turned to

Bob Paradise, who Buffler describes as "someone who walks in the room, and you love him right away." Charming and personable, Paradise's role was to help persuade landowners of the merits of this initiative. Hockey and horticulture—who knew?

Ultimately, about 80 percent of the 85 private riverfront landowners agreed to a deal. Initial funding would come from the St. Paul, McKnight, Mardag, and F.R. Bigelow Foundations, as well as from the Helen Lang Charitable Trust, the State of Minnesota and a knot of corporations that included H.B. Fuller, the *St. Paul Pioneer Press*, and Arthur Andersen. Great River Greening would arrange volunteer labor and administer the program. In return, landowners would let Great River Greening plant on their property, and they would maintain the plantings. The various parties negotiated to balance the needs of property owners, such as signs, sight lines, and security, with the city's desire that the area be attractive and authentic.

But in Coleman's mind, the greening program was more than about trees, it was about people making a commitment to their city. In his mind, every person who dug a hole and planted a tree had a new stake, in this case quite literally, in the future of the city. Volunteer getting their hands dirty became a metaphor for people caring.

"We got volunteers by running articles in the papers and running really good events," Buffler says. "Our events are very well organized—we tell people when to come, what to bring, and what to wear. Plus we provide bathrooms, food, and trained supervisors, who are also volunteers." As a result, Buffler says, "People were able to come down and apply their volunteer labor in an intensive way, and when they were done they had these tangible benefits that they could see. I think that's why we were really popular. It was fun, and there was a sense of hope with all the neighbors working together for the community. They love it, and we do, too." Great River Greening still puts out a newsletter for volunteers, encouraging them to roll up their sleeves for future events.

By May 2001, 10,000 volunteers had put around 35,000 trees and shrubs into riverfront land, at a cost of about $4 million. The Greening project's success in St. Paul has enabled it to spread its influence throughout the region, now applying its technologies and practices in the St. Croix and Minnesota River valleys as well.

The next step in Coleman's plan was overhauling the infrastructure. St. Paul has more Mississippi river bluff than any other city, but by 1994 there was literally no place downtown a person could get to and stand alongside the river and gaze. The area's infrastructure had been designed with the needs of railroads and other industry in mind; not much thought had been given to allowing ordinary citizens to gather at the water moving through their midst.

Worse, what infrastructure was already in place looked bad. St. Paul riverfront roads, bridges, and other public works projects were about as dispirited and down at the heels as the river itself. Pitted concrete and rusty steel discouraged investors and business owners from putting money and effort into the downtown area. Navy Island, the funny little island occupying choice space alongside the Wabasha Bridge, needed to be "stormed and liberated," in Dick Broeker's words.

In renewing the riverfront's infrastructure, the city had several goals in mind: making the river more accessible to St. Paul's citizens, improving the riverfront's appearance, and by meeting the first two objectives, attracting new business and investment.

St. Paul wanted people to live, work, and play closer to the river, so their first objective was to make sure that citizens and their property were safe from storms and floodwaters. To do this, in 1995 the U.S. Army Corps of Engineers completed a $22 million floodwall and esplanade that reaches the length of the Great River Park, from the St. Paul Airport to the High Bridge. In good weather, the esplanade feature allows St. Paulites to stroll alongside the river, away from the rush and bustle of traffic.

Shepard Road, for decades a mainstay of traffic in the metropolitan area, followed every twist and turn of the river. Its location made it convenient for the needs of railroads and other industry. But the busy four-lane road also made it difficult for pedestrians to get to the Mississippi. "Shepard was like a concrete dam that separated you from the river," Broeker says. "If people can't go down to the river and put their feet in it, you're never going to bring the riverfront back."

So the city pried Shepard Road away from the river, creating a buffer zone of green for the river area, making it quieter and more attractive; it also created the real estate necessary one day for possible housing and other urban development along the Mississippi at that point.

To make the river even more accessible, the city installed a $1 million public dock and gazebo, stretching 500 feet downstream from Harriet Island. That dock was finished in time for the summer of 1995, and attracted boaters and visitors of every stripe.

Revitalizing the core

"But we should not squander this once-in-a-lifetime opportunity. Therefore, I will continue to call on the corporate community, the foundations, private citizens, other levels of government, and neighborhood groups to work with me in revitalizing the urban core."
—Mayor Coleman, State of the City Address, February 1997

Next, the Coleman's team turned its sights on Harriet Island itself. The island, on the river's west bank near Wabasha, was an undervisited wasteland of slag parking lots and rundown picnic facilities. "At the south end of Wabasha is Harriet Island, ready to reclaim its historic role as the city's community gathering center," the mayor said. "I will work aggressively to rebuild Harriet Island as a true waterfront park and regional destination center, restoring Wabasha Street and Harriet Island, creating housing opportunities."

With the leadership from Riverfront Corporation board members Jay Cowles and Pat Donovan, the community choose to condense a 15-year plan for rebuilding Harriet Island down to a three-year campaign of raising money, gaining necessary regulatory approvals, and generating an inspiring design. The private sector rose to the challenge, contributing more than $5 million including $125 contributions from more than 2000 individuals who wanted to leave their permanent mark on the community. "Stepping Stones," brick pavers with personalized inscriptions, gracing Harriet Island's new promenade reveal the community's pride in its waterfront birthplace. Megan Ryan, the city's marketing director, calls it a case of "capitalizing on the affection people feel for St. Paul."

It seemed that everyone wanted to have a hand in bringing Harriet back to life. Here are just some of the organizations that pitched in: The St. Paul Companies, Target Corp., Wells Fargo Bank, the St. Paul Foundation, the Katherine B. Andersen Fund, *Star Tribune*, MAHADH Foundation, Firstar Bank, McGough Construction, Hugh J. Andersen Foundation, U.S. Bank, Benis Company, F.R. Bigelow Foundation, Mardag Foundation, *St. Paul Pioneer Press*, the City of St. Paul, Dellwood Foundation, Helen Lang Charitable Trust, McNeely Foundation, St. Paul Firefighters Local 21, Knight Foundation, Ecolab Inc., 3M Foundation, Mary Livingston Griggs Foundation, Marbrook Foundation, Peanuts on Parade, The Beim Foundation, TKDA, Ramsey Medical Society, The Bayport Foundation, NSP (Xcel Energy), SRF Consulting, St. Paul Port Authority, the Frey Foundation, St. Paul Convention and Visitors Bureau, and Regions Hospital. A long list, but it isn't complete.

Today, with the bandages removed following its reconstructive surgery, Harriet Island is a friendly expanse of green where once there was only litter and cement. Jogging and biking trails invite visitors to circumnavigate the island's dimensions. Picnic tables, gazebos, a playground, a band shell named for Target Corp., and community events on the island promise to make Harriet Island a place families spend the day at again. For those with a slightly more formal evening in mind, the island now boasts the Mildred Pierce, a restaurant serving upscale continental food. On the St. Paul side of the river near Harriet Island, Joseph's serves family-style fare. Step aboard a permanently moored barge and you are in a brand new bed and breakfast, the Covington Inn. Soon, Harriet Island will be home to more than a million visitors a year.

If the properties at river level needed help, so did the infrastructure above it. Coleman inherited a wobbly Wabasha Street bridge that threatened to direct motorists to the bottom of the river instead of across it. Until that happened, it wasn't much to look at, either. Years earlier the city commissioned a plan for a new bridge from renowned architect Jamie Carpenter; that bridge would have cost $75 million, completed. The city didn't have that kind of money, and it had no luck convincing businesses to chip in for the project. "St. Paul was bleeding so badly that they didn't want to put money into the waterfront because they couldn't see the relevance to downtown," Broeker says.

But now Coleman had their attention. Seeing all the other changes, and believing that a revived riverfront would be good for downtown business, merchants agreed with the mayor that a new bridge would contribute to a new and improved city. So the coalition started over from scratch, commissioning a new, less expensive bridge plan from a city/community design firm that included architectural firm TKDA. The resulting Art Deco-style bridge that was opened in 1998 now serves as a fanciful landmark and visual delight to the four lanes of motorized traffic that pass over it every day. The refurbished link also includes bicycle and foot traffic lanes, as well as improved access to Raspberry (formerly Navy) Island. "We didn't just build any bridge," Ryan says. "We built a beautiful bridge."

In the future, the city and its coalition may turn other former industrial sites into public projects. There's a possibility that the Lift Bridge will be turned from a railroad bridge into a bike trail, once the railroad no longer needs to use it, says Riverfront Corp. executive director Seeb. The transformation of the riverfront has everyone seeing the city in a new way. Liabilities become assets. Eyesores are inspirations. "Part of the role of the Riverfront Corp. is to see things not as they are," Seeb says, "but as they could be."

Anchors by the river

"Riverfront development is about revitalizing the urban core. It has brought hope and investment to the heart of the Capital City. Its focus spreads beyond the river itself—and will result in a reenergized Wabasha Street—from the West Side over the new bridge, right up to the steps of the State Capitol."
—Mayor Coleman, State of the City Address, February 1996

Coleman's vision was rapidly gathering steam. Littered lots became green parkland. Roads were rerouted, bridges rebuilt. But to be successful, the riverfront needed something special, a world-class reason for going down there. It needed at least one large, indoor destination site that would attract visitors and residents alike and form a physical connection binding the downtown to the river.

One of the first victories for Coleman's resettlement efforts was attracting Lawson Software from downtown Minneapolis. Coleman's vision was that the city had a jewel at its heart, the river, and that was something other cities would kill for. Bill Lawson, chairman of Lawson Software, was one of the first to glance up and see that Coleman was on to something. The focus of that attraction? That knowledge workers like software developers need to let off steam, and the riverfront made an exquisite jogging track for professionals fighting burnout and depletion from long hours. The move of Lawson to a sensational new office building in St. Paul more than made up for the departure of West Publishing.

But the city still needed a killer attraction, a charismatic presence about which the population of the entire region would sit up and say, "Hey, I need to get over to St. Paul and check that out." It happened that the Science Museum of Minnesota had been looking for a new building since 1992, to replace the Cedar Street quarters it had outgrown. The museum was exactly what the coalition was looking for as an anchor attraction. In addition to its regular and special exhibits, the Science Museum is a scholarly resource through its collections and research programs, the site of the second Omnitheater in the United States, and a traveling educational resource for schoolchildren, with five vans and an army of educators that serve classrooms throughout the upper Midwest.

In the early 1990s, museum administrators realized that the existing building, located on the northern end of downtown, couldn't accommodate the number of visitors who wanted to come, nor the space to store its collection of 1.75 million objects. Educational programs were bumping up against space shortage, too. "It's kind of an interesting problem—it's coping with success," notes Kathleen Wilson, who has spent the past eight years as the museum's vice president of planning and external relations.

The museum was committed to staying in St. Paul, the city where it had begun in 1907. But museum officials were not initially enthusiastic about building on the downtown side of the river. "They did not want to come over to the downtown side of the river because all their marketing studies said people didn't want to come visit them downtown," Broeker says. With some arm-twisting from Coleman and other coalition members, however, the Science Museum eventually agreed to build in its current location. "I mark this as the major turning point in Coleman's political life," Broeker says. "He played a card that was very dangerous. He essentially said, 'If you come over to our side of the river I'm going to support you and get you a lot more money. And if you stay over there you're not my friend.'"

Coleman got the Science Museum the money it needed to build a new building, and museum administrators became happier about the move. "Science happens all around us, not just inside buildings, and we thought it would be wonderful to have some exhibits outdoors," Wilson says. "The Science Museum's mission is telling stories, and the river has many stories to tell—anthropological, archeological, environmental, and we thought it would be wonderful to locate near the river." The riverfront location has also allowed the Museum to have a boat, the River Eye, which does environmental scanning on the Mississippi.

The Science Museum finalized its plans in fall 1994 and broke ground in the spring of 1997. City and state funds, as well as donations from private citizens, fueled the new construction, to the tune of about $100 million. On Dec. 11, 1999, the museum held its grand opening, and it was a grand opening. People from across the region swarmed to the new quarters. In the fiscal year that ended June 30, 2001, the Museum had 925,000 visitors, and served another 200,000 through educational outreach programs. "The Science Museum has been a key component in riverfront development and in the residents' perceptions of the river and its use," says museum President Jim Peterson. "It's been a centerpiece in the midst of a lot of other activity and has called a good deal of attention to new uses of the riverfront."

An urban village

"And now as we are experiencing a remarkable economic and community renaissance, the Mississippi River will continue to provide the energy. For the first time in a generation we can look at adding 300 to 400 housing units in our downtown and riverfront."
—*Mayor Coleman, State of the City Address, March 1999*

St. Paul's original settlers lived along the river, and the coalition to recreate the city was eager to see a new generation of settlers there. Creating a residential enclave beside the purling waters was a good investment in several ways, they decided. First, people would want to live there, because it was a beautiful place. Second, it was a convenient place to live for downtown workers. Third, the arrival of new people would itself be a stimulus to downtown business, as shops and restaurants sprang up to serve the growing community.

And so a plan took shape. New housing would be grouped into three distinct urban villages. The first, the North Quadrant, is the furthest along in its development plan. It will eventually consist of eight to ten blocks downtown, with 900 housing units, retail businesses, and a new public park.

The second planned grouping, the Upper Landing project, will stretch for about 25 acres along the river between Chestnut Street and the High Bridge. After spending about $12 million on remediation for the site, Texas developer Centex Corp. plans to put 600 housing units there. The Upper Landing was St. Paul's historic Italian settlement village, turned refuse site. Soon it will be home to 600 families, building on the already vibrant West Seventh neighborhood. Wrapped with bike trails, green spaces, and retail shops, it will become a new gateway into St. Paul's entertainment district.

Ground already has been broken on the third premier urban village, the West Side Flats. Beginning with a U.S. Bank office development, this new neighborhood will include townhomes, apartments, and condominiums in the area between Wabasha, Robert, and Plato Streets. Like the other urban villages, however, it will include walking and biking trails and retail outlets when it's completed by St. Paul developer JLT West Side LLC.

The riverfront-based fix-up will touch other parts of downtown as well. Lowertown, which has benefited enormously from urban renewal during the past decade, will continue to get new coats of paint. The city hopes to spend $4 million renovating the farmer's market, adding indoor, year-round facilities. "It's 20 years old—it simply needs to be refurbished," says Seeb. Other Lowertown priorities include moving the post office and renovating Union Depot, which both the city and Amtrak would like to use for train service.

One big question remains: Will the next mayoral administration see to it that these projects—some of which are little more than a blueprint and a shovel—come into being? Coleman believes they'd be foolish not to. "I don't think they have a choice," he says. Expectations are high. Deals are in place. The incentives to continue are enormous.

And, says Seeb, "It's what the community wants. That trumps all, doesn't it?"

It's about people

"In recent years the river has been at the center of the revitalization of St. Paul. But it's about more than projects, it's about people."
—Mayor Coleman, State of the City Address, March 1998

From auspicious beginnings of riverfront clean-ups and family fishing events, Coleman always returned to a central theme: "Cities are about people." Whether it was the American Smithsonian, the Ramsey County Fair, or Minnesota Orchestra concerts under the stars, Coleman always looked for ways to engage, involve and include people of St. Paul and the region.

And even his riverfront planning effort found a way of engaging thousands of citizens over hundreds of meetings. When the "St. Paul on the Mississippi Development Framework" was unveiled in June of 1997 it was greeted by standing-room only crowds who responded with standing ovations. "I have spoken at a dozen conferences around the country," says Seeb. "No city can tell the same story of community support for a planning process." Coleman had tapped into pent-up demand in the community.

The demand was more than about planning, it was a demand for action, for participation, and for enjoyment. That was a theme Coleman returned to again and again. What do we do in the city of St. Paul? We live here. What do we expect from the experience? Satisfaction. Engagement. Happiness.

The Grand Excursion

"And so this evening, I ask you to join me on our journey as we begin a walk into the future. I call it St. Paul: Vision 2004."
—Mayor Coleman, State of the City Address, March 2001

In his final State of the City speech, Coleman presented his vision for where St. Paul was headed and what it could achieve by the year 2004. "The Mayor operated on a belief that you had to inspire people to greatness, then work to get something done, something tangible, tomorrow," says Seeb. "For him, the Grand Excursion was a vehicle to keep people headed in a direction while navigating the challenges of day to day life."

They say that simple satisfaction is the proper reward for a job well done. But the public/private team that envisioned and then enacted this remarkable dream of a city revitalized by the river flowing through it, plans to cap it all with a fabulous perk—a recreation of Millard Fillmore's ballyhooed 1854 riverboat trip from Rock Island to St. Paul.

That original trip was billed as a journey into America's heartland, and featured the president and a small army of dignitaries and journalists. The journalists—who knew a good press junket when they saw one—filed stories in virtually every major American newspaper about the river, about Rock Island and St. Paul, and about the towns they traveled through along the way. The stories they wrote fired the imagination of the entire country, about this romantic outpost on the frontier, and helped propel the territory of Minnesota to statehood.

The recreation of the Grand Excursion, as it was called, will take place in 2004. It will celebrate the work that has been completed in St. Paul and the entire region at that point, and help generate extra energy for whatever projects are yet to be completed. As Norm Coleman says, "There are always dreams that don't have a shovel." The Excursion will also celebrate the re-greening of America's heartland and the part that St. Paul has played in the resurgence.

Building Blocks

*Norm Coleman and the Capital City Partnership
revived commercial real estate in downtown
St. Paul with a few key moves.*

BY SUZY FRISCH

Bill Lawson was expecting the pitch of a politician: a hard sell on the greatness of St. Paul and an offer of financial incentives to lubricate the wheels of the deal. But when Norm Coleman and Capital City Partnership President and CEO John Labosky arrived at the first-floor conference room of Lawson Software's building in Northeast Minneapolis to meet the CEO, Coleman mostly just asked questions about the company: What exactly does Lawson Software do? What are your space needs? Coleman left some brochures about St. Paul, and told Lawson he hoped he would find a potential fit for his company there.

Afterwards, Coleman and Labosky walked through the halls of Lawson Software, shaking hands with employees and talking with them about St. Paul.

That meeting changed everything for Lawson—and for St. Paul. Throughout 1996, Lawson Software had been scouting suburban locations across the Twin Cities, looking for space where it could stretch out. The software development company was growing at a 50 percent annual clip, and employees and executives seemed to think a campus environment would be the best place for it to continue its success.

"We hadn't thought much about downtown St. Paul until [developer] David Frauenshuh introduced us to Norm Coleman," recalls Lawson. "I hadn't met very many politicians, so I didn't know what to expect. But he was bright, intelligent, and interested in learning about what Lawson was and if there would be an opportunity there that would fit both of us. It got us thinking."

Lawson and his 800 employees got more interested in moving to St. Paul when Coleman came to the company's Christmas party to talk up the city—the entertainment, the restaurants, the excitement of being in a vital urban center. Soon, Lawson says, employees started inquiring, "Why don't we move to downtown St. Paul?" Bill Lawson was finally convinced when the mayor came back to the company to explain his vision for revitalizing St. Paul with Dick Broeker, at the time the head of the St. Paul Riverfront Corp., and Pam Wheelock, who was then the city's director of Planning & Economic Development.

"He talked about what potential was there. He felt like St. Paul was on the move, and there was a lot of commonality with Lawson there," says Lawson. "He talked about the additions to the riverfront, the Science Museum, the nightlife, the restaurants, the shopping, the hockey stadium—things we weren't used to in the suburban community. He described what it was like to be there. We have a young kind of group of people at Lawson Software who liked the community aspects of getting involved with people outside of Lawson. They liked the restaurants and the Starbucks. The younger people thought it would be great."

But the question remained: If Lawson came to downtown St. Paul, where would it go? Coleman and Labosky had in mind one block of prime St. Paul real estate across from Rice Park, but it was particularly run-down. The block—bounded by St. Peter, Wabasha, Fifth and Sixth Streets—had what was probably the only failed McDonald's in America, a parking garage, a small grocer, and a handful of other small businesses. The group toured several sites downtown along with Frauenshuh, who was interested in redeveloping the block.

"It was a fairly ugly block," Lawson recalls. Anticipating this reaction, Labosky and his staff at the Capital City Partnership created a computerized 3-D tour of the city (funded by Partnership member 3M) that erased all of the blight and put a shiny new skyscraper in its place.

Lawson and other top executives eventually were sold on the move—contingent on Frauenshuh and the city negotiating a deal to raze the block and pave the way for Lawson's headquarters. Lawson and Coleman sealed the deal with a handshake. In 2000, after many hurdles and a brief political firestorm over St. Paul stealing a business from Minneapolis, Lawson Software moved into its new 13-story headquarters, and downtown St. Paul had a new addition to its skyline. Lawson also brought 1,100 employees to downtown who were never there before, and gave St. Paul a company that boasted $300 million in annual sales—with aggressive goals to reach $1 billion in sales in two to four years.

Getting Lawson to move to downtown St. Paul was a major coup for Coleman and the Capital City Partnership, and it caused a sea change in the way things were going in the commercial real estate sector. "The Lawson building was huge," says Don Garofalo, president and CEO of Andersen Corp. in Bayport. "It symbolized in a very public way that St. Paul's renaissance was for real."

Labosky agrees. "Lawson was a landmark project," he says. "It gave the real estate community confidence in St. Paul as a venue. Every deal after that was much easier to do because Lawson was here. It helped us tremendously. A series of high-tech firms moved downtown because Lawson was there."

City-building, brick by brick

Attracting Lawson Software was particularly important to St. Paul because it halted the deterioration of the city's center and got it back on track. Not much had been going well in St. Paul for many years, and the commercial real estate picture downtown was especially bleak in the early 1990s. What's more, just when things were starting to look good for Minneapolis after the real estate glut of the early 1990s, vacancy rates soared to 20 percent in downtown St. Paul in 1994. At the same time, downtown property values had tumbled from a high of $677 million in 1988 to $298 million in 1994. "Businesses started to leave, and the image of the city got tarnished," says Labosky. "People thought St. Paul had no future, especially compared to Minneapolis."

Worry about St. Paul was deep enough among Twin Cities' executives that they were willing to pitch in however they could. St. Paul Companies CEO Doug Leatherdale, the founding chairman of the Capital City Partnership, gave the newly recruited Labosky a place to hang his hat when he started the job in April 1996. "I was very concerned with what was happening with downtown St. Paul," says Leatherdale. "We needed to bring Twin Cities CEOs together to do something. We wanted to put together a plan for how we could begin to rejuvenate what was a clearly a decaying downtown. A facelift was needed for this city. We needed to encourage people to stay and encourage people to move here."

On his first day on the job, Labosky got flooded with calls from nearly 100 people, including 14 commercial leasing agents. They desperately wanted him and Coleman to talk to their tenants and convince them to stay in St. Paul. For months, Coleman and Labosky went all over downtown, meeting CEOs and talking with them about their vision for St. Paul. Their vision was this: Minnesota's capital would be a vibrant river city that used the Mississippi as a recreational and environmental asset, not just as an industrial thoroughfare. They visualized mix-used developments that brought people to live, work, shop, and come for entertainment in downtown. They wanted a cleaner and brighter downtown, safer streets and skyways, and more reasons to encourage businesses to relocate and expand in St. Paul.

"It goes back to my theory that if you generate confidence and create movement, things will start happening," says Coleman. "I remember going with Dick Broeker to talk to Bill Lawson about riverfront development, about being in an urban center where you could walk across the Wabasha Bridge to Harriet Island for an ice cream social, about the possibility of having an NHL team here. And he bought into the vision. We had pieces moving in the right direction. We had a clear vision of what we wanted to do and what could be done. Bill Lawson understood that vision— and that it could be done."

Addressing commercial real estate was the first step in realizing that vision. Coleman and the Capital City Partnership had to work on retaining the employers that were already there, and get new companies to move downtown. To that end, Coleman spoke to anybody who would listen about his plan to make St. Paul an exciting place to live and work. Throughout 1996, Labosky and Coleman met with scores of CEOs. Ultimately, many of them decided to keep their businesses in St. Paul. Slowly, their campaign began to work. In 1996, the city absorbed 363,000 square feet of office space, the highest absorption rate in St. Paul's history, notes Labosky. And things only got better.

Moving up

Around the same time that Bill Lawson and Norm Coleman were shaking hands on Lawson Software's move to St. Paul, other good things started to happen in the commercial real estate sector. The city's bedrock corporations began to make decisions to expand their headquarters in St. Paul, including insurance giants The St. Paul Companies and Minnesota Life, as well as Ecolab, the global marketer and manufacturer of specialty cleaners and chemicals. Others, such as Bloomington-based Health Partners, decided to move into the city or expand operations there.

Leatherdale and The St. Paul Companies played a major role in sealing the Lawson deal and helping Coleman and the Partnership fulfill their mission of attracting and retaining major businesses. Lawson, with 1,100 employees by the time the Lawson Commons was ready in 2000, could not fill the 13-story building by itself. The financing for the project was such that all of the space needed to be filled for it to work, and the deal was on the verge of collapse. In stepped Doug Leatherdale and The St. Paul Companies.

"Because Lawson was a privately held company, it didn't have the ability to do the deal by itself and get the necessary financing," recalls Coleman. "It couldn't fill the whole building. I remember calling Doug Leatherdale at home, telling him about this opportunity, and saying we needed The St. Paul to lease some of the floors. We talked about the importance of making this work, and he said, 'Yeah, lets make this thing happen.'"

The St. Paul Companies agreed to take at least 100,000 square feet of the space for six years, until Lawson needed the extra room for its own expansion plans. For Leatherdale, the move reaffirmed a decision the company had made in the mid-1980s to stay downtown. Despite signs that St. Paul was floundering, The St. Paul Companies made the tough choice to build a new corporate headquarters in the city instead of heading for the suburbs. "We stayed in St. Paul then because we've been here for almost 150 years. The name of the company and the name of the city are synonymous," says Leatherdale. "We have about 1 million square feet of real estate, and we decided it was the right decision to stay in the city and not build a suburban campus. It was still the right decision when we needed to expand."

While the Lawson/St. Paul Companies deal was being sealed, Ecolab was facing a tough decision of its own. Ecolab CEO Allan Schuman says his ever-growing $3 billion company was being courted to relocate into non-tax states like Florida and Texas, as well as other metropolitan areas. "Everybody was coming to us," says Schuman.

It was an appealing prospect. Ecolab needed more space than what was provided by its existing headquarters at 370 North Wabasha, and offices in the old NSP building at 360 North

Wabasha and the Capital Centre at 386 North Wabasha. Schuman had to figure out where Ecolab should expand. Should the company leave the city where it was founded in 1923 and prospered, to take advantage of the lucrative tax breaks and incentives offered by other cities and states? Or should it remain in a city with marginal weather and high taxes? The choice seemed obvious.

Ultimately, though, Schuman decided that Ecolab should stay put and expand directly across the street from its existing headquarters, spending $12 million to renovate the interior and exterior of the Capital Centre. Why? Schuman cites two key reasons: an obligation to his employees, and Norm Coleman. "I've been with Ecolab for 44 years, and I've built up a very strong affinity for the work ethic of our people and the loyalty they show the company, so why screw around with them? We have an obligation to our people," says Schuman. "Norm's a good salesman as well. What did he say? 'Don't go!'"

Ecolab fashioned an urban corporate campus in the heart of downtown at Fifth and Wabasha Streets. In addition to its headquarters building, the campus includes Ecolab University, a global training center for its sales and service employees. In addition, the newly renovated Capital Centre helped make room for 600 new employees. Ecolab also helped beautify the area with a towering steel and acrylic sculpture that it unveiled in 1999.

Schuman credits Coleman especially, and the Capital City Partnership, as keys for turning around the commercial real estate market in St. Paul. "I don't care what anybody says, it's Norm. It's leadership," he notes. "We were looking at other areas—parking is no bargain and rent downtown is costly. There are a lot of places to go. Here's a salesman saying, 'Don't leave St. Paul. I'll make it a little better city for you.' And that's what the Partnership did, too."

A top corporate citizen

Minnesota Life had a similar decision to make. From 1995 to

1997, CEO Bob Senkler had been deliberating about what the company should do about its space needs, and exploring options outside St. Paul. Yet his heart really wasn't in a move. He didn't want to disrupt the lives of the company's employees; 26 percent of Minnesota Life workers lived in St. Paul, and almost half of the employees carpooled or took the bus to work.

Plus, ever since the company was founded in 1880 it had been located in St. Paul. There was a deep history and connection with the capital city that Senkler didn't want to abandon. "Being a good corporate citizen is important to us," says Senkler, "but you can't ignore the economics of a move elsewhere. At the same time, having a good economic package that helped the city of St. Paul was important to us, too."

Other factors came in to play. A feeling that good things were happening in St. Paul, that it was a city on the move, was palpable around town, and Senkler took notice. He learned that Lawson Software had committed verbally to becoming a St. Paul resident. He also was excited about the new Science Museum of Minnesota being built along the Mississippi River, and the new Minnesota Children's Museum going up along West Seventh Street. New restaurants were opening, and there was talk of getting an NHL team to play at the old Civic Center.

When it came down to it, the City of St. Paul made it worth the company's while to stay downtown, Senkler says. The city paid for razing the block bounded by Minnesota, Robert, and Sixth Streets, and Seventh Place, with a $15 million loan from Minnesota Life. Senkler credits the St. Paul City Council and Coleman for their leadership in realizing the importance of keeping Minnesota Life downtown, and he praises the Capital City Partnership for facilitating communication between the parties and helping seal the deal that kept the company downtown. "[The fact that] the City of St. Paul was serious about retaining this company made it a pretty easy decision," says Senkler.

Senkler and Minnesota Life decided to build a new 13-story building in St. Paul, across the street from its headquarters at

Sixth and Robert Streets. Not only did it add 571,500 of Class A office space to downtown St. Paul, the $102 million building also brought with it a daycare center, a police substation, and a parking ramp. The company, which is one of the largest employers downtown with 2,400 workers, had outgrown its 20-year-old building and was leasing space around downtown St. Paul. The new building would provide it with a new headquarters, consolidate scattered employees into one location, and allow the company breathing room for future growth.

The goal of bringing more major companies to downtown St. Paul got another boost in 2000. U.S. Bancorp, after searching around the metro area—including the suburbs—at 30 different locations, picked the west side of downtown St. Paul as the place to build a new operations center. Coleman pursued the project with intensity, flying with Jack Grundhofer on the CEO's private jet to Los Angeles to buttonhole him about St. Paul.

It was another case of Coleman and the Partnership gaining success by being a cheerleader for the city. "The bank agreed to come to St. Paul because of all the good things that were happening. They liked the idea of being a part of a renaissance along the river," explains Brian Sweeney, director of St. Paul's Planning & Economic Development department. "The Capital City Partnership was very helpful in coordinating the bank folks to make sure they were part of the negotiations and discussions. Our shop [Planning & Economic Development] did the negotiations to complete the deal with U.S. Bank, but John Labosky was very helpful at various points to make sure it was moving forward."

The new facility is part of the West Side Flats, a $79 million mixed-use development with 500 units of upscale housing rising on the west side of the Mississippi River. The 350,000-square-foot U.S. Bank operations center is expected to bring 2,200 employees to work at the facility. "It's an incredible project that is great for the city," says Coleman. "It's about personal relationships and working with people, having the partnership and being at the table. And it's because success begets success."

A confidence-building move

It could be argued that getting Lawson Software to move to St. Paul was the one big coup that bred many more commercial real estate successes downtown. It's the story of a business leaving the city where it was founded in 1975 and picking St. Paul as the place to continue its growth and expansion. And that was a confidence builder that made many St. Paul residents sit up and say, "Maybe we do have something to offer."

Not only did Lawson build confidence, it also helped put St. Paul's downtown back on the road to fiscal health. So did the expansions by Minnesota Life, Ecolab, and The St. Paul Companies, and new offices for many other businesses. In all, $1.7 billion in new investment since 1998—in infrastructure such as roads and bridges, new buildings, new housing, restaurants, and more—has helped turn things around for downtown.

The numbers tell the story of the rebirth of St. Paul since the creation of the Capital City Partnership in 1996: employment in downtown has gone from 45,343 people to 51,360 in 2000 (the last year for which final numbers are available), a 13 percent increase. In 1996 alone, the market absorbed 363,000 square feet of office space, meaning that the space got leased. After a sharp decline in absorption rates in 1998 while office space was torn down to make way for the new Lawson and Minnesota Life buildings, 518,882 square feet of space was absorbed in 2000. And by 2000, vacancy rates for space downtown in all classes had fallen to 8.1 percent, down from that 20 percent figure in 1994.

The renaissance in downtown St. Paul's commercial real estate sector started with a vision. If leaders can restore confidence that St. Paul is a world-class city, and show people that they mean business with cleaner streets, a safer downtown, and better amenities, business leaders will feel that confidence, too. And if you involve executives in making changes for the positive— through public-private organizations like the Capital City Partnership, for example—they'll typically make decisions for their companies that further the mission of the city.

Bill Lawson and his executive team bought into the vision. They wanted their employees to have opportunities to be out and about in the community, and to have choices of things to do after work. "There are a couple of reasons why we decided St. Paul was the right place to be," says Lawson. "At the top of the list was the way Norm Coleman described the city. He led us to believe there was a good opportunity here, and showed us that it's a very good city."

Walking around downtown with Coleman brought back fond memories for Lawson of when he first moved to Minneapolis from Wichita, Kansas. He and his brother, Richard, would meet for lunch and people-watch. It was nothing like Kansas. "I had never experienced a downtown before. We'd buy lunch and stand around in the street to see what was going on. There was activity, and it was fun," remembers Lawson. "As our young people at Lawson got more interested in downtown, some of those memories came back, and I think it had some impact. We could see the energy building downtown."

Bill Lawson is now retired from Lawson Software, but new president and CEO Jay Coughlan believes the decision to move to St. Paul was the right one for the company. "St. Paul has been very good for Lawson, and the main reason is because it's been very motivating for our employees," he says. "The rank-and-file people enjoy working here. They enjoy the buzz that the city has. There are more places to eat; you can walk around. It's an environment that helps the employees feel better about coming to work, and they're more productive."

Lawson Software still hasn't filled up all of its space in Lawson Commons, but the building was designed so that the company could expand when necessary. At the rate Lawson is growing, it won't be long. That's a vision anyone would be happy to see.

Slap Shot

A team of business leaders led by the Capital City Partnership helped bring professional hockey back to Minnesota—in St. Paul.

BY SUZY FRISCH

After two years spent pursuing a long-shot dream of getting a professional hockey team for St. Paul, Mayor Norm Coleman and the city were inching closer to making it happen: St. Paul learned it had made the NHL's list to be one of four cities to get a new pro hockey franchise. So on a cold, gray day in April 1997, the city played host to a contingent of NHL team owners and executives to show off the capital city and the deep support in the community for a new professional hockey team.

Part of the visit included a tour of the old St. Paul Civic Center to prove that an updated version of the 30-year-old building could accommodate a new team. Robert Naegele Jr., the majority owner of the Minnesota Wild, recalls the day. "There were no leaves on the trees and the wind was blowing, and it was probably representative of the feeling that everybody had about that old bomb shelter [the Civic Center]," remembers Naegele, who led Rollerblade to enormous success and whose family founded the Naegele Outdoor billboard company. "There were no windows and it was dark. As we walked in, we were greeted by the residue of what had taken place there the day before—the circus. As they were sweeping up, the fumes of elephant dung were wafting to the ceiling."

It wasn't a good sign—or smell. Coleman had pinned his hopes for a team on the belief that it would cost the city only $30 million to renovate the Civic Center, not upwards of $130 million to build a new state-of-the-art stadium. But that probably couldn't happen now. Vance Opperman, now an owner of the Wild and CEO of Key Investment Inc., recalls hearing NHL Commissioner Gary Bettman tell the St. Paul group that there was no way the NHL would grant the city an expansion team if it had to play in an old arena like the Civic Center.

But as Coleman says, getting the Minnesota Wild was a deal that nearly died a thousand times. And this was just one of them. There were other elements that impressed the NHL officials about St. Paul: the deep and substantial support of the local business community—in the form of a coalition led by Doug Leatherdale, CEO of The St. Paul Companies and the founding chairman of the Capital City Partnership. This coalition, with the Partnership playing a major role, ultimately convinced the NHL that support for pro hockey in the Twin Cities was extraordinarily deep. The league granted St. Paul the franchise. Eventually, that same coalition won the uphill battle to gain some of the funding for a new arena from the Minnesota Legislature, which for years had been unfriendly to helping pay for other sports facilities. In the end, they were victorious on both fronts.

How did it all come together so winningly, in only three and a half years? Certainly, key factors were the strong and undying support of the business community, and Coleman's obsession with bringing a major entertainment venue to downtown St. Paul. "Norm was an amazing guy through all of this," notes Leatherdale. "There were incredible obstacles, and everyone said it couldn't happen. He didn't believe that. Anytime you were going down a road and it would be blocked, he would have a new idea. He just didn't give up."

Adds Coleman: "Some deals are about vision and some deals are about money. But some deals are about providence: And this was a deal that just wouldn't die."

How deep is the well?

As the NHL Board of Governors headed to St. Paul to scout out the city, the league was having its doubts about the Twin Cities. The metro area already had three professional sports teams—the Vikings, Twins, and Timberwolves—that local businesses backed through sponsorships and luxury suites, as well as a major Division I university. Would there be enough support, and money, for another professional team?

John Labosky, president and CEO of the Capital City Partnership, got word of these concerns before the NHL group arrived, and he had already gone to work. He gathered letters from 50 CEOs, who pledged their support for the potential hockey team to the tune of $100,000 a year for five years for luxury suites. When Bettman and his contingent got to the boardroom of the St. Paul Companies for a presentation about the merits of St. Paul as a potential expansion city, he asked Labosky directly whether there was enough corporate money to go around to back up a fourth professional sports team.

Labosky recalls saying to Bettman, "Gary, I can't honestly say whether we can support four major teams and the University of Minnesota over the long term, but I can demonstrate that businesses will support hockey in St. Paul," and he handed over the letters. "That's as far as I had to go," he adds. "The Timberwolves weren't going anywhere, but we all understood that it would be a challenge to support baseball and football without building them a new stadium. But all the NHL had to deal with was whether we could support hockey. And clearly we could."

Jac Sperling, CEO of the Minnesota Wild, credits this early support from the business community and the members of the Capital City Partnership for selling the NHL officials on the St. Paul team. "Early on, Doug Leatherdale galvanized the business community to support Norm's vision about the possibility for returning the NHL to Minnesota, and especially St. Paul," Sperling says. "Labosky supported that and helped us talk to the business community and potential suite holders. They helped us with initial efforts in garnering support in the business community. They helped foster confidence in the city that this might be successful and that St. Paul is a good place to be, and that's where hockey should be."

The NHL agreed, and Labosky ended up being right about the business community's deep backing for professional hockey. But it wasn't an easy task convincing anybody that pursuing professional hockey was feasible, or the right thing to do.

Calling an entertainment anchor

Where did the idea come from to bring professional hockey back to Minnesota—and in St. Paul for all places, which had never hosted a professional sports team? When Coleman and business leaders formed the Capital City Partnership, they developed a five-point plan for revitalizing St. Paul—"city-building," as Labosky likes to call it. Step one was retaining existing companies and attracting new ones to the heart of St. Paul. Things were starting to look up on that front: Development along the Mississippi was progressing, the Science Museum had decided to stay in St. Paul, and the commercial real estate sector was improving.

The next step, once the employment base expanded, was to give people reasons to stick around after work or to come downtown on the weekend. Labosky recalls that he, Leatherdale, and Coleman were sitting around one day talking about downtown St. Paul. "We decided we needed a major entertainment anchor downtown," he says. "We thought, 'Let's get hockey back.'"

They believed that the team could play in a renovated Civic Center, which was practically sitting empty at that point. Professional hockey would be the answer to their quest for foot traffic.

NHL hockey's 43 home games a year would mean more than 750,000 people streaming through St. Paul on nights and weekends during the season. And events on more than 100 other days and nights at the renovated arena could attract nearly 2 million people.

The idea was solidified, and Coleman and the Capital City Partnership started on their mission to bring hockey to St. Paul. Even so, the quest for professional hockey came in fits and starts, starting with a flirtation by Richard Burke to move his Winnipeg Jets team to the Target Center or the Civic Center. When that didn't work out, Coleman tried getting Hartford Whalers owner Peter Karmonos to move his team to St. Paul. And while that was being discussed, Coleman kept his options open and cold-called Gary Bettman at the NHL to ask the league to consider St. Paul for a team. He told Bettman that the state was ready for hockey again, three years after the Minnesota North Stars bitterly left the state for Dallas in 1993.

Upon the recommendation of Burke (who ended up moving the Jets to Phoenix), Coleman contacted Jac Sperling. A Denver attorney who specialized in sports transactions, Sperling worked on the deal that had moved the Quebec Nordiques to Denver to become the Colorado Avalanche. Sperling came to St. Paul to meet Coleman, despite misgivings that the effort to bring hockey to Minnesota was a huge long shot. "As he has done with many people, he is very persuasive," says Sperling. "His faith and confidence was contagious." Sperling agreed to help the St. Paul effort.

But many questions remained unanswered about the team. Was it feasible to renovate the Civic Center? And would the Twin Cities economy support a new professional hockey team? Studies needed to be done to evaluate the Civic Center, and consultants such as Sperling needed to be hired. But Coleman couldn't spend city dollars on an effort to attract a professional sports team.

In stepped the Capital City Partnership, which put up the money to pay for the necessary studies and consultants. "The Partnership was very, very critical in the beginning," says Coleman. "It became clear early on that in order to do this we needed a lot of money up-front. This was a dream that few people believed, except the business community and the Partnership. They funded all of our initial effort, our demographic studies, and facility review studies, $400,000 of their own money—none of it public."

A team without owners

Despite this progress, one crucial piece still was missing: The potential hockey team had no owners. Throughout the early days of the effort to bring hockey back to Minnesota, Coleman, the Capital City Partnership, and other business leaders publicly stood behind the project. But they were a city in search of a hockey team they would never own themselves. St. Paul needed private investors. So Coleman, Sperling, Leatherdale, and Ecolab CEO Al Schuman started working on gathering together investors to line up behind the project. They talked to anyone who would listen—business leaders from both sides of the river, members of prominent St. Paul families, stalwart hockey boosters.

In the summer of 1996, Coleman took Naegele to breakfast to tell him about his idea for a professional hockey team and to see if he would be interested in backing the effort financially. Later, Naegele's son, Robert Naegele III, asked his dad what he thought of Coleman's idea. "I told my son, 'I think he's a total and complete dreamer. But let's not dismiss it,'" recalls Naegele.

Around that time, Coleman also called Opperman, whose family had been a mainstay in St. Paul as owners of West Publishing, to see if he could tell him about his plan for hockey. He wanted Opperman to become the lead investor for the team, the person who would be the public figure in support of the quest to win back professional hockey. "He wanted an effort to bring hockey back to Minnesota, and I told him it was a bad idea," says Opperman. "The North Stars had lost money, and there was no appropriate place for a team to play."

Opperman did, however, agree to come to meetings that were being held with potential investors and other hockey supporters. The group started holding regular meetings in an attempt to keep things moving forward. Sperling was usually there, and sometimes Ray Chandler, an architect from HOK Inc., the St. Louis firm that built Coors Field in Denver for the Colorado Rockies baseball team, in addition to many other stadiums. He also had agreed to be a consultant on the project.

Occasionally the younger Naegele would attend and report back to his dad about the progress. By the time the elder Naegele returned to St. Paul from his home in Naples, Fla., in early 1997, matters were moving along at a fast clip. The city was ready to submit an application to the NHL and head to New York City to present it. Problem was, the coalition needed to firm up a lead investor. After consulting with his wife and children, Naegele agreed to do it. "It was a noble and valiant effort, and a chance to do something of historic value," says Naegele. "How many opportunities does a man have in his lifetime to be a part of that?" Eventually, after hearing pitches from Sperling and Coleman, 13 other investors signed on, including Opperman and broadcasting magnate Stan Hubbard.

Naegele, along with Governor Arne Carlson, Coleman, Labosky, Sperling, and others traveled to New York City to present their application. Their bid was met warmly. Soon after, St. Paul learned that they had convinced the NHL; the league announced that the city had made the short list of candidates for expansion teams. Things were looking good.

And then the NHL came to town for that fateful visit in April 1997. That's when the group learned that Coleman's dream of renovating the Civic Center was dead. If St. Paul wanted a professional hockey team, the NHL said, it would need to build an arena for the 21st century.

That raised new challenges. The group would now have to ask the Minnesota Legislature for money to help build a new $130 million facility. The group knew how much luck the Twins and

Vikings had had with their own proposals. But the hockey coalition didn't have much wiggle room, either. Time was waning on the 1997 legislative session, and the NHL was going to make a final decision soon. Without the crucial funding commitment of the legislature, the NHL was going to pick another city.

The hockey lobby

Fortunately, the hockey boosters had Carlson on their side. That much was obvious when he went along with Coleman and others to New York to help pitch the NHL on St. Paul (other cities just had their mayor along). Now the group had to win over the recalcitrant legislature. Unfortunately for the hockey folks, 1997 was not a bonding year, and the legislature didn't want to open the can of worms that was funding for professional sports facilities. Not only that, Coleman was running for reelection against State Senator Sandy Pappas, and she and her supporters weren't exactly racing to hand the mayor a political victory. The debate about providing funding for a new professional hockey arena lasted until the last night of the session in May 1997.

"I remember laying in bed listening to the radio to the debate on the floor," recalls Coleman. "We had nine days to have a firm commitment to have an arena built, and we had to have all the money on the table, and we didn't have it. We didn't have the $65 million we needed from the state. I remember going to sleep thinking, 'This deal is dead.'"

The next day, Coleman called NHL Commissioner Bettman to warn him of the bad news and to ask for another week to pull things together. Things didn't look good, and the hockey boosters knew it. "We needed the financial commitment from the legislature," says Naegele. "We were quite dejected after the legislature adjourned with no help for us. We had spent several hundred thousand dollars on a very worthy effort—on travel, and legal, and design. But it seemed to me that it was for the most part a failed effort."

But new inspiration struck Coleman the following morning,

when he woke up with the idea to have the city guarantee the money for the arena. He arranged a meeting with Carlson and won the governor's commitment that he would include the $65 million in the bonding bill in the next session—the state's share of the $130 million arena. Minnesota would loan St. Paul the $65 million in interest-free loans, and it would forgive $17 million of that if the arena would host public events every year. The city also contributed $65 million in bonds, and the team would pay the building costs for the arena, along with $6 million a year in rent and taxes. A few days later, the St. Paul City Council went along with Coleman's idea and voted 6-1 to guarantee the $65 million. Jubilant, the mayor immediately called Bettman to tell him that an arena would be built in St. Paul.

Victory came about a month later, on June 17, 1997, when the NHL announced that St. Paul would be home to one of the four expansion teams, along with Atlanta; Columbus, Ohio; and Nashville, Tenn. St. Paul held a ticker tape parade, and a giddy Coleman rode through downtown St. Paul on a Zamboni ice machine. The team, eventually named the Minnesota Wild, was scheduled to start play in 2000.

But the fight still wasn't completely over. St. Paul needed the Legislature to include funding for the new arena in the 1998 bonding bill. When lawmakers convened to work on the bill, there still was a lot of work to be done to convince legislators to approve the state's $65 million for the arena. Pam Wheelock, who was then director of the city's Planning & Economic Development department, spent many hours at the Capitol talking to lawmakers about hockey. As a key negotiator on the issue, she repeatedly made the argument that a new facility was good for St. Paul and the entire state. "We were removing an aging facility that would soon become a liability to taxpayers of St. Paul and replacing it with an asset," says Wheelock. "We also talked about a relative commitment the state was making [to expand] the convention center in Minneapolis. There was a pretty well-orchestrated effort to build public support for the project."

Still, the debate over the arena came down the wire. Up until the last minute, legislators were balking at funding the new facility. Fortunately for Coleman and the St. Paul coalition, Carlson was on their side, threatening to veto the bonding bill if the $65 million for the Minnesota Wild was not included in the measure. "I remember being holed up in the governor's office all day and all night on the last day of the session," says Coleman. "The clock was ticking, and [Senate Majority Leader] Roger Moe wouldn't agree. At one point the governor, who'd been great, said, 'I don't think it's going to work out.' About a half an hour later, Roger said we had a deal. In the end, people couldn't walk away from having an NHL franchise. No one wanted to be the bad guy."

Game on

Now that professional hockey was going to be a reality in St. Paul, the Wild wasted no time in getting started putting the team together. The day after St. Paul was granted the franchise in June 1997, the team was open for business in its office in Suite 2000 of the Piper Jaffray Plaza, and was taking deposits for season ticket reservations. After three business days 6,000 people had put down $100 for a nonrefundable season ticket. Ultimately, 16,000 season tickets were sold, attesting to the enthusiasm the community already felt for a team that wasn't even going to be playing for another three years.

The Twin Cities business community and the populace at large got so enthusiastically behind the Wild that it led the new team to a hugely successful launch. Details of that success include selling out all 74 of the Xcel Energy Center's luxury suites in just eight weeks; selling all 2,800 season tickets available on the expensive club level; and selling out every one of the team's 43 home games in the first season. The kickoff of the Wild was better than anyone could have imagined.

It's these ardent Wild fans that Coleman, Labosky, and others dreamed of seeing visit St. Paul on evenings and weekend to watch professional hockey played in the capital city.

71

While the fans have kicked off the new hockey team with a bang, they also have played an integral role in transforming a core part of downtown St. Paul. Not only are the hockey-goers and other visitors to Xcel Energy Center spending money on tickets, they also are regularly patronizing existing restaurants and bars, as well as the many new establishments that have cropped up along West Seventh Street and elsewhere in St. Paul during the past few years.

Before the hockey team started to play at the Xcel Energy Center in the fall of 2000, West Seventh Street used to be a rather desolate place. There just wasn't much to draw people there apart from a handful of small, unassuming bars and diners. But the anticipation of having more than 18,000 people flood the area on 43 nights a year spurred many business people to take a new look at the area. They figured, "Why not jump on the Wild bandwagon and provide some new eateries and watering holes for all of those hungry and thirsty hockey fans?"

That's what led business people like Pat Boemer, owner of the sports bar Patrick McGovern's, to add a second floor to his tavern, and Moe Sharif of the Downtowner Cafe to turn his low-key diner into an upscale eatery called the Downtowner Woodfire Grill. It's why new restaurants like the Vine Park Brewery and The Wild Tymes Bar and Grill opened up near the Xcel Energy Center. And it's what has helped fill upscale restaurants like Pazzaluna and Kincaid's night after night. These fans and the Minnesota Wild are also why scores of restaurants and bars have hopped on the Capital City Trolley's game plan, which allows ticket holders to Wild games to park and dine at their establishments, leave their car in the lot, and take the trolley to the Xcel Energy Center, and back after the game. It's a brilliant way to increase business—and reduce post-game traffic jams.

Having the Minnesota Wild in St. Paul has made a huge impact on other downtown St. Paul businesses, too. Some hotels have undergone renovations to accommodate the many new customers, and others are in the works. Additionally, other downtown St. Paul hotels have noticed a substantial increase in business when the Wild are in town. Hundreds of the Wild's season ticket owners come to St. Paul for games from South Dakota, Wisconsin, and outstate Minnesota places like Rochester, St. Cloud, and Mankato. Often, those fans spend the night in St. Paul and make a big event of the game rather than making the long trek home. The Radisson Riverfront Hotel and the Saint Paul Hotel both attribute increases in room rentals and restaurant receipts to the presence of the Minnesota Wild. (Visiting hockey teams typically stay at the Saint Paul Hotel.)

The Wild intentionally marketed season ticket sales to areas outside of the Twin Cities, and the St. Paul Convention and Visitors Bureau has picked up on the idea. On its Web site, the bureau offers package deals to St. Paul that can include game tickets, a hotel room, tickets to the Minnesota Science Museum, and a shuttle to the Mall of America. These weekend visitors make a huge economic mark on St. Paul as they stay at local hotels, eat at area restaurants, shop at stores in St. Paul, and visit other cultural attractions in the city.

And actually, St. Paul had started gaining benefits from the Wild even before the team had ice to play on in the city. Just planning for the team and building the new arena helped fatten the city's coffers. The Capital City Partnership commissioned a study a few years back by accounting and consulting firm KPMG to evaluate the potential effect of a hockey team on St. Paul. The firm found that the construction of the arena alone would cause $44 million in direct spending in St. Paul and $74 million in additional economic benefits for the city—a total of $118 million. Additionally, KPMG estimated that if the Wild had an operating budget of $60 million, St. Paul would see $18 million in direct spending and $31 million in additional economic benefits—a total of $49 million. Finally, KPMG determined that the Wild's estimated $60 million operating budget would lead to the creation of 3,677 full-time jobs in Minnesota, 2,321 of which would be in the city of St. Paul. The new jobs, and the new spending in St. Paul certainly have and will have a large ripple effect in St. Paul. They will go a long way toward furthering city leaders' goals of revitalizing St. Paul.

New confidence

Gaining the nightlife in downtown St. Paul and the extra economic benefits from the Minnesota Wild undoubtedly have helped St. Paul's fiscal health. But the hockey team has given the city an ego boost as well. Landing the Wild was another confidence builder for St. Paul, one that led to more decisions by business leaders to stay in the city, expand their companies there, or move their businesses to St. Paul. Says Coleman: "It was the recognition of St. Paul as a major league city."

Winning the Wild and the getting the state-of-the-art Xcel Energy Center built has meant everything to revitalizing St. Paul, notes Brian Sweeney, the city's director of Planning & Economic Development. "It has completely transformed St. Paul," he says. "People who haven't been back in five years cannot believe the new St. Paul. It's not the moribund city that we had five years ago—the street life, the business life, the entertainment life, all have completely changed downtown."

For Coleman, the Wild have brought on a more personal satisfaction. He recalls driving down West Seventh Street after the Wild's first exhibition game. "It was 11 p.m. and the streets were overflowing with people. I couldn't have imagined the change in the atmosphere in St. Paul, the intensity of the warm feeling that it created. This was a different St. Paul."

That's what Coleman, Leatherdale, Labosky, and other members of the Capital City Partnership were aiming to do when they set out to get a professional hockey team for St. Paul. They knew intuitively that giving people an exciting reason to come downtown after work and on weekends would mean the resurgence of their city. They were right.

Cultural Renaissance

St. Paul's arts and cultural institutions—long a core strength of the downtown area—found new life and new audiences during the city's resurgence.

BY CHRIS MIKKO

Not everyone realized it at the time, but Saturday, Sept. 10, 1994, was a watershed date for St. Paul. On that late summer afternoon, the St. Paul Chamber Orchestra (SPCO) put on a free performance in a rather unusual location: aboard a 140-foot barge moored off of Navy Island, in the shadow of downtown. Skeptics had predicted a light turnout. But when SPCO Music Director Hugh Wolff took the stage a little after 1 p.m., he looked out at more than 8,000 people who had settled in on the banks of the Mississippi for the concert.

The huge crowd testified to the drawing power of two of St. Paul's finest assets: classical music and the Mississippi River. One of those assets—music—had been nurtured and supported over the years. Since its founding in 1959, the SPCO had become one of America's premier chamber orchestras. As for the Mississippi, well, that was another story altogether. Decades of industrial abuse had transformed downtown's stretch of river into a barren, abandoned waterway, walled off from the city center by railroad tracks, Shepard Road, and a concrete levee. Still, it retained a powerful mystique. As the concert revealed, people loved the SP-CO. They wanted to love the riverfront, too, but it wasn't always easy.

When Norm Coleman had taken office earlier in 1994, he had brought up the prospect of forging new links to the Mississippi. That idea didn't sit well with some people in town, many of whom worried that a riverfront-based strategy would divert energy from the city's current arts-based marketing campaign. You see, St. Paul had been trying to position itself as a cultural mecca for years, highlighting its stellar lineup of arts institutions, which featured such heavyweights as the Ordway Center for the Performing Arts, the Science Museum of Minnesota, and the Minnesota History Center. It also had number of smaller, but no less vibrant community-level organizations—including the Penumbra Theatre, Park Square Theater, and the Great American History Theater, to name a few—and a thriving artist's community in its Lowertown neighborhood.

There was only one problem with the approach: It wasn't working. The city's tourism numbers were flat, retail development was stagnant, and downtown resembled a dead zone after 5:30 on weekdays, and all through the weekends.

Hence Coleman's emphasis on forging new links to the riverfront, which would serve as the focal point for a newly revitalized St. Paul. In his view, riverfront development would strengthen the entire city, including its arts and cultural institutions. "It was an inclusive view of city-building," he explains. "We approached [downtown development] with the fundamental belief that the city is a natural gathering place; we had a plan to create an environment in St. Paul where people would work, play, and live. We understood that the 'play' part was a key piece of that equation—people play with the Ordway, with the Minnesota Children's Museum, with the Minnesota Museum of American Art, with hockey arenas."

As that plan unfolded over the next few years, it became apparent that St. Paul's arts and cultural institutions wouldn't be neglected. In fact, they emerged as key factors in the city's revival—and found a wealth of new audiences in the process.

Cultural confusion

The early 1990s were grim days for St. Paul. Downtown was in a long, slow decline, and none of the city's redevelopment efforts seemed to be working. In July 1990, West Publishing, one of St. Paul's oldest and most stable employers, fled downtown for a new corporate campus in Eagan—rejecting a sweetheart package of financial incentives and a massive riverfront office complex plan proposed by the city. The city's retail environment—the bulwark of its 1980's-era growth strategy—was drying up. Galtier Plaza and Town Square, a pair of mixed-use shopping mall projects that had opened to great fanfare just a decade earlier, were bleeding tenants. And rumors were swirling that Carson Pirie Scott and Dayton's, downtown's last remaining department stores, were itching to leave as well. (The Carson store would be gone by 1993.)

In early 1991, with no clear solutions emerging, St. Paul looked to one of its traditional strengths—its arts institutions—for economic salvation. That year, the city endorsed the "Cultural Corridor," a plan to link up several dozen cultural attractions that were scattered around downtown. Backers theorized that such a district would lure visitors to the city—and spur economic development in the form of small shops, restaurants, bookstores, coffeehouses, and the like. They also hoped that it would position St. Paul to compete for tourists against Minneapolis and the soon-to-be completed Mall of America. The city's endorsement wasn't just lip service, either: St. Paul allocated 10 percent of the annual revenue generated by its half-cent sales tax—roughly $750,000 per year—to development in the corridor.

As promising as it seemed, the plan was hindered by some serious flaws. For starters, there was the problem of physical identity. While its name suggested a dense clustering of arts venues, all within walking distance, the "corridor" actually covered an area bounded by Cedar Street on the east, Kellogg Boulevard on the south, John Ireland Boulevard to the west, and I-94 to the north. Most of its attractions were located a good distance apart from each other, and one, the Minnesota History Center, was cut off altogether from downtown by I-94. The corridor's roomy boundaries also made for some jarring streetscape contrasts. A few blocks from the understated urban elegance of Rice Park, visitors would encounter the weary environs of Wabasha Street, home to the forlorn and mostly empty Wabasha Court building, an "adult novelties" store, and the almost surreal site of a long-shuttered McDonald's restaurant.

Worse yet, few people knew about it. A *St. Paul Pioneer Press* poll completed in the summer of 1992 revealed that less than 11 percent of all residents in the Twin Cities' East Metro knew what the Cultural Corridor was.

Nonetheless, St. Paul kept launching new efforts to promote the Cultural Corridor to wider audiences. And, to be fair, some of its attractions probably did benefit from the attention. The Ordway fortified its position as a national-caliber performing arts venue. The Science Museum consistently drew big crowds (and in mid-1992, began searching for land to build a larger facility). The Fitzgerald Theatre, buoyed by the return of Garrison Keillor's *A Prairie Home Companion* radio program, rose to new prominence. And, with the city's help, a coalition of arts groups began holding twice-yearly "art crawls" that showcased the work of downtown artists, and drew hundreds of attendees.

But, by the mid-1990s, the cohesive district that planners had envisioned had yet to materialize. The lack of retail development was particularly disappointing. Apart from a small, short-lived coffeehouse on St. Peter Street, and Sakura, a popular Japanese restaurant that moved from Galtier Plaza to the corner of Sixth and St. Peter, the heart of the corridor remained much the same as it had four or five years earlier. A person who came downtown to, say, visit the Fitzgerald, had few post-show dining or shopping options, and thus little reason to stick around.

Jeff Nelson, the city's director of Cultural Development, and a longtime observer of the city's art scene, says the corridor suffered from bad timing. "By its nature, a lot of cultural-type activity happens indoors—behind the walls of museums and galleries. To create a really vibrant cultural district, you need arts venues plus a lot of other activity: great restaurants, brightly lit shops, people out on the street having a good time," he notes. "When the corridor concept was set up, downtown simply didn't have enough critical mass of those other elements. The corridor was marketed before the city could support it."

Coleman's assessment is slightly more blunt. "Were we going to be able to build a city through culture alone? No," he says. "However, we understood that we could use culture as one of the tools to build the city."

Links and icons

If anyone was questioning the Coleman Administration's commitment to St. Paul's cultural environment, much of that doubt was erased during the summer of 1995. On July 13th of that year, the St. Paul City Council agreed to a deal that paved the way for the Science Museum to build a new facility on the banks of the Mississippi River in downtown. Under the agreement, the city would acquire the new site, and invest millions to renovate streets in the area, clean up the site's soil, and make a variety of other site improvements. St. Paul's total commitment: $15 million.

The decision was a major victory for Coleman, who had been working vigorously on the project for more than a year. When the Science Museum's leaders had initially leaned toward building on a site across the river from downtown, Coleman had personally persuaded the museum to stay in the city center. He had also helped convince a number of corporations and foundations to contribute millions to the museum's construction fund; the presence of those donations ultimately helped sway the city council—never an easy sell—when it came time for its final vote.

Coleman was sure the Science Museum was worth the effort. On one hand, it had been a longtime pillar of the local economy, employing 300 people and attracting 800,000 visitors annually to downtown. The new museum would also provide a sparkling new cultural icon for the city, a tangible acknowledgment of the importance of arts and culture to downtown St. Paul. While the old building had been tucked into an isolated spot on the corner of Cedar and Exchange, the new site was on a prime piece of real estate along Kellogg Boulevard, directly across from the River-Centre special event/entertainment complex, and a few blocks away from Rice Park. Designed by the Minneapolis-based Ellerbe Becket architectural and construction firm, the building's plan called for a 370,000-square-foot facility (roughly double the size of the old building) that would house the nearly 2 million objects in the museum's collection, and offer a state-of-the-art line-up of interactive exhibits, live theater presentations, science demonstrations, and films. In short, it would be a bold addition to downtown's cultural scene—and, museum officials and city leaders hoped, an attraction that would draw at least 1 million visitors per year.

In addition, the new building would create a significant physical and symbolic connection from downtown to the river. Visitors would enter the museum by crossing a 50,000-square-foot plaza off Kellogg. Once inside, they would find glass walls offering sweeping views of the Mississippi, along with a central stairway that stepped down to a network of exhibit halls on the museum's different levels—and, ultimately, to a 10-acre park at the river's edge. The plaza, central staircase, and park would all be open to the general public, and used for a variety of events such as concerts and festivals.

City leaders understood that the new Science Museum would be a powerful addition to the city's cultural and physical landscapes. But few believed that it could cure downtown's woes by itself. It was a single icon, and as Coleman is quick to point out, "we we're not going to make St. Paul vibrant by a single icon—we needed a more holistic vision for the city."

The power of art

By the time Coleman had kicked off his second year in office, he'd already assembled a broad-based team that was laying the groundwork for that vision. The team—which included representatives from various city departments, area businesses, nonprofit foundations, and citizen's groups—came up with a five-part urban redevelopment plan. In a nutshell, it went something like this: First stimulate commercial development. Then develop and market entertainment and cultural attractions to draw people to the city. Next, cultivate a residential population that would drive retail growth. In sum, the idea was to create large-scale momentum that would build on itself, and eventually create the elusive "critical mass" that Nelson, the city's cultural development director, refers to. Coleman's redevelopment team—the "Development Cabinet"—began meeting every other Friday morning to piece together how to make the steps in the plan happen. Each member of the group, Coleman says, was charged with "taking a specific piece of a project and doing what they needed to do to make the thing a reality."

According to Capital City Partnership President and CEO John Labosky, arts and cultural institutions were a frequent discussion topic at the meetings. "We realized that they provided St. Paul with unique, one-of-a-kind attractions that allowed this city to compete favorably with Minneapolis and the suburbs," he explains. "We needed them as part of the overall plan for downtown. People will come to St. Paul specifically to see the Science Museum or to go to the Minnesota Children's Museum—but not for suburban-style retail."

Labosky and the Partnership aggressively promoted and nurtured St. Paul's cultural environment over the next few years. On a broad scale, the group highlighted the city's arts and cultural institutions in its printed promotional materials. It also gave them significant space on its Web site, which features a sophisticated events calendar and database; users can quickly track down detailed information on a wide range of arts institutions—everything from the Ordway to the Penumbra to the E.M. Pearson Theatre on the Concordia University campus.

The Capital City Partnership also reached out to local arts organizations. For example, it gave a direct grant to Public Art St. Paul, a local nonprofit, to help produce a 26-page brochure detailing public art projects around St. Paul. Along with Ecolab Inc., it helped fund the creation of "Skygate," a $225,000, 52-foot-tall, lighted, walk-through sculpture erected on the Ecolab Plaza along Wabasha Street. The help wasn't only in monetary form, however. Jane Eastwood, the Science Museum's vice president of marketing communications and sales, recalls how the Partnership held a series of sessions with downtown arts institutions, offering marketing ideas and strategies on how the organizations could cross-promote their offerings. One direct result of those sessions was "Tuesday Tourist," a promotion in which 20 museums and galleries offered free admission to downtown employees each Tuesday during the lunch hour. As Eastwood notes, the campaign worked, thanks in large part to the Capital City Partnership's help. "They were invaluable," she recalls. "They helped us plan out how the promotion would work. They posted information about it on their Web site. And they got us in touch with the right people at local businesses so we could tell their employees about it."

Meanwhile, the city continued its own support of arts and cultural projects. A few examples: In mid-2001, it completed a $750,000 renovation of a metal sculpture and the pedestrian apron around the Rice Park fountain. As part of its $14.5 million restoration of Harriet Island Park, St. Paul built new docking facilities for the University of Minnesota's Centennial Showboat, which will be used by the University of Minnesota's theater arts program for public performances beginning in summer 2002. And along the Seventh Street Place pedestrian mall between Wabasha and St. Peter, the city helped pump new life into the old Orpheum Theater. In the summer of 1999, a developer purchased the long-shuttered, 1,750-seat building from the St. Paul Port Authority and restored its original name: the Palace Theater. In January 2001, the Brave New Workshop, a Minneapolis-based theater troupe, signed a four-year lease to put on an interactive, Irish-themed play called "Flanagan's Wake" in the theater's lobby. The city helped out with a $75,000 grant that went toward a splashy new neon marquee for the front of the building, and a separate $45,000 grant that helped the building's owner defray the costs of renovating the structure. The results were far better than anyone could have hoped for—"Flanagan's Wake" played to sold-out audiences throughout 2001.

The city's "Peanuts on Parade" initiative also fit into the arts and cultural category—and revealed the power of art as an economic development tool. During the summers of 2000 and 2001, hundreds of polyurethane Snoopy and Charlie Brown statues, all sponsored by local businesses, were put on display at various locations in the city. The statues proved wildly popular with the public, and often drew steady streams of visitors. At the same time, however, they also served the local arts community in a number of ways. All of the statues were painted and decorated by local artists; the Capital City Partnership Web site featured detailed statements by each artist on his or her inspiration for the design (along with a wealth of information on where visitors could find statues around town). And the City of St. Paul and St. Paul's College of Visual Arts set up the Blockhead Gallery, a temporary venue in a vacant storefront on Wabasha Street that exhibited other examples of each statue artist's work.

"Better angels"

Today, a mere seven years after the SPCO's riverfront concert, downtown St. Paul looks and feels like a far different city. There are now 8,000 more employees in the central business district. Tourism is up significantly—from 3.46 million visitors in 1994 to more than 5 million in 2000. New commercial buildings such as Lawson Commons, Xcel Energy Center, and the recently completed Minnesota Life building dot the skyline, and commercial property values have appreciated by nearly 100 percent.

It also has a stronger, more cohesive, and far more visible arts and cultural environment. Along Kellogg, the new Science Museum has been living up to its advance billing as a regional tourist destination, drawing nearly 1 million visitors in 2001 alone. A few blocks away, on the corner of West Seventh and St. Peter, the flamboyant, purple- and orange-walled Minnesota Children's Museum has transformed a spot once occupied by a notorious bar and, later, by an asphalt-covered parking lot. The new Lawson Commons building on Wabasha houses two coffee shops and a bookstore. A number of new restaurants—Pazzalunna, Great Waters Brewing Co., Kincaid's—have been added to the city center. Even the long-depressed Seventh Street Place shows signs of new of life. In addition to the Palace, it also is home to Park Square Theater, a pair of restaurants, an art gallery sponsored by the College of Visual Arts, and a number of small shops.

In short, the goals of the old Cultural Corridor idea—attract more visitors to the city, fuel economic growth, create street-level activity—are being realized. The city now has the beginnings of a true cultural district, one that offers visitors a variety of things to do and see.

All of this is not to say that the city's work is done—most observers agree that there are still areas in downtown desperately in need of renewal. But it does illustrate the power of Coleman's "holistic" vision of city-building. It took the riverfront-focused master plan—and the combined efforts of the public and private sectors—to begin to restore new life to downtown. At the same time, it also shows the unique power of arts and culture as an economic development tool—they lend a richness and texture to the urban environment that, as the Capital City Partnership's Labosky notes, give St. Paul a unique identity.

Coleman agrees. "I keep coming back to the idea of cities as gathering places," he says. "We needed the arts as a key piece in making St. Paul into a true gathering place. Maybe its my 1960s 'good karma' thing that still floats out there, but I believe that the arts appeal to the better angels in people. If people feel good and are uplifted by the arts, they act in a good fashion. And that is what this city—any city—needs."

A Community Effort

St. Paul's neighborhoods give strength, cohesiveness, and stability to the capital city—and when one area needs help, everyone steps in.

BY JACQUELYN B. FLETCHER

For years, many Twin Citians have viewed Payne Avenue, a major north-south artery in St. Paul's East Side neighborhood, as a grimy street that offered little enticement to residents or visitors to stop and shop. Unless, of course, you were interested in visiting the Payne Reliever, a notorious neighborhood strip joint. For more than two decades, the bar showcased nude dancers and the occasional fistfight among patrons. That changed at the end of 1999, when a local developer named Jerry Frisch bought the building and the land with the aid of grants and loans from the city and closed down the Payne Reliever for good. With that, the neighborhood took a huge step in the redevelopment of the long-blighted street. It wasn't the only step, however. In recent years, Payne has started on a remarkable turnaround, and is fast becoming a vital commercial center.

In fact, the entire East Side neighborhood is regaining the identity it enjoyed in the middle years of the 20th century—as an area that features solid, affordable housing; plentiful jobs; and a strong sense of community. The East Side has not been alone in such efforts, either. Many of the city's neighborhoods—from Thomas-Dale to Macalester-Groveland to the West Side—have been building their own success stories in the last few years. According to Bryan Sweeney, director of St. Paul's Planning & Economic Development department, the city's neighborhoods have seen approximately $1.8 billion in new investments over the last half-decade (compared to $1.7 billion in downtown during the same period).

It's no accident that such investment is happening. St. Paul has long been known for its neighborhoods—a bunch of enclaves that feel like a collection of small towns, each with their own unique ambience. That individuality stretches back to the city's earliest days. St. Paul began as a French settlement in the 1840s, and originally was divided into two distinct sections created by breaks in the river bluffs. The primary spot was Lambert's Landing—also known as the Lower Landing or today, Lowertown—which was the first site encountered by boats coming up the Mississippi. The secondary site was called the Upper Landing, and was located at the foot of what is now Chestnut and Eagle Streets, near Seven Corners; it had its own business and residential district known as Uppertown. By the 1850s, increased river traffic was bringing more people to the settlements, including settlers who gradually filled in the surrounding area.

Over the years, the communities took on their own character. For example, the West Side, across the Mississippi River from downtown, has long been home to a vibrant mix of different cultures, including Eastern European Jews and Italians, and later, Latin Americans. Merriam Park was born in the 1880s as a suburban enclave offering train service between the downtowns of Minneapolis and St. Paul. St. Anthony Park, now a well-to-do residential community tucked into the northwest corner of St. Paul, grew out of a primarily industrial area. Dayton's Bluff, a community built on rolling terrain overlooking the east side of downtown, started as a wealthy residential locale, but a population boom in the late 19th century brought in a wave of blue-collar residents. "Our neighborhoods are the core fabric of this city; they are an integrated urban mesh," says St. Paul Mayor Norm Coleman. "St. Paul is a big small town. And one of the great thing about small towns is the quality of life. People know each other. They see each other on the streets. That's what we've worked to create."

Capital City Partnership President and CEO John Labosky agrees with that view. "St. Paul's neighborhoods are the envy of many cities around the country," he says. "They're safe, affordable, clean, livable, and ethnically diverse.

"The destinies of downtown and its surrounding neighborhoods are intertwined," Labosky adds. "Downtown may be the heart of the city, but its neighborhoods are the extremities; one can't survive without the other. A big part of our mission has been to reconnect downtown with its surrounding communities, and to support the neighborhoods in their own development efforts."

That support actually has come in a variety of different forms, from a variety of different sources. Under Coleman's leadership, the City of St. Paul has taken an aggressive role in neighborhood-building. Consider, for instance, Coleman's "Development Cabinet," which meets every other Friday morning. Among others, the group includes representatives from the St. Paul Riverfront Corp., the Capital City Partnership, and a variety of city departments: Planning & Economic Development, Public Works, Parks & Recreation, the RiverCentre, and the St. Paul Port Authority. The team approach has proved its worth over the years, as the urban renewal process has brought with it a host of complicated challenges—everything from assembling deals with developers to rallying community support to solving zoning issues to cleaning up heavily polluted "brownfield" areas.

In a similarly assertive fashion, the Partnership has also reached out to neighborhoods with funding for projects and marketing help. Area businesses and foundations have provided financial assistance. Local citizens' groups have done the work at the grassroots level. In short, neighborhood development in St. Paul has been a community effort, one that has seen a broad consensus of people roll up their sleeves, strive to figure out what's missing and what they can do to bring about positive change.

A road will run through it

At the end of the 18th and beginning of the 19th centuries, trains were still the main form of transportation for big industries in the United States. Train tracks running from downtown St. Paul and through the East Side brought large manufacturers to the area and ensured jobs for the skilled laborers living in the neighborhood. Many of those laborers were from immigrant families. The East Side has long been a haven for newcomers to the United States; in the last century, it has welcomed new residents of Irish, Swedish, Italian, African, and Polish heritage. More recently, Latino and Hmong families have flocked to the area.

However, as trains were exchanged for trucks during the last century and old manufacturing technologies gave way to new, the economic status of the neighborhood plummeted. The area lost a number of key employers—including the Whirlpool Corp., which pulled out in the 1980s, and the Stroh's Brewery, which shut down its East Side operations in 1997. Over the past 25 years the area has lost approximately 2,500 jobs, and unemployment levels have climbed as high as 17 percent. With money leaking out at such a rapid pace, the formerly robust area became a scarred wasteland of hulking, empty buildings; contaminated land; run-down housing; and dispirited residents.

Something had to give. In 1994, a group of representatives from 3M, Wells Fargo, the City of St. Paul, and local community development corporations such as the East Side Neighborhood Development Co. (ESNDC) began discussing ways to help. By 1995 enough interest and money was raised to staff the Phalen Corridor Initiative, a group that has developed partnerships with area companies, business associations, and the city (Coleman headed its advisory committee). The idea of the Phalen Corridor was born to help develop jobs and opportunities in the neighborhood, in part by creating Phalen Boulevard, a new, 2.5-mile road along the old railroad line that runs through the heart of the East Side. Construction will begin in 2002 and will occur in two phases. Phase one—which will link the new Williams Hill Business Center industrial park to Payne Avenue—should be complete by 2004. Phase two—Payne Avenue to Prosperity Avenue—is projected for completion by 2010 or sooner.

Of course, there's more to it than just building a road. The land along the old railway corridor also needed to be developed for future use. There was a big problem with that plan, however. The corridor was rife with brownfields—areas in which the land had been contaminated by long-term industrial usage. With the city's direct assistance, the Phalen Corridor Initiative has been working to clean up and restore the area. To date, it has rehabbed more than 60 acres, with more than 100 acres still needing to be decontaminated. The plan is to develop the area with business parks, medium-density housing, and greenspace—all of which will foster a sense of community and bring new prosperity to the area. "The fact that we have utilized the detriments of the neighborhood is a key to what we are doing," says Curt Milburn, executive director of the Phalen Corridor Initiative. "We've taken the problems and turned them into opportunities for the future."

The results are showing. Case in point: The Williams Hill Business Center on the area's west end. Built under the direction of the St. Paul Port Authority, the 25-acre industrial park houses six companies that employ more than 650 people, all of whom make at least $14 per hour. What's more, the Port Authority plans to build another industrial park on yet another brownfield along the corridor; construction on the 22-acre site is slated to begin in 2003. The neighborhood also boasts a new Metro Transit bus garage that anchors the west end of the corridor and which supplies both jobs and access to the area. At the east end of the corridor, the new offices of the Minnesota Bureau of Criminal Apprehension and a new Wells Fargo branch will open in 2002. Nearby, on York Avenue, the John A. Johnson Achievement Plus Elementary School opened in 2001 in a formerly abandoned warehouse. The school, which overlooks the central portion of the Phalen Corridor, shares its space with a new YMCA facility.

According to Milburn, these and other new developments have already created 1,000 new jobs—"and we haven't even really started yet," he adds.

New gains for Payne—and beyond

One sector of the Phalen Corridor, Payne Avenue, has made its own redevelopment headway in recent years. In 1998, the ESNDC launched an ambitious community revitalization initiative. Known as the Payne Avenue Main Street Program, the effort is the result of a variety of groups—including the Payne-Arcade Business Association, District 5 Planning Council, East Side Arts Council, and the City of St. Paul—working together. The idea was to remake Payne Avenue based on the national Main Street model, which had been developed 20 years ago by the National Trust for Historic Preservation and the Local Initiative Support Corp., two organizations devoted in part to preserving neighborhoods by fighting the effects of "big" development. "Small towns were being devastated by the Wal-Marts going in," says Katya Ricketts, director of the Payne Avenue Main Street Program. "We need to save the historic buildings. We have to make them economically viable. The model works so well because neighborhoods are like small towns. It's a hybrid program that we are combining with our knowledge of urban development."

The program got a boost when the Payne Reliever closed in December 1999. After the city agreed to help finance developer Jerry Frisch's project to turn the bar into a delicatessen and bingo hall, the old street began trying on a new look—one inspired by the tenets of the Main Street Program. One key component of that has been to improve the appearance of the buildings along the street. In 1999, the ESNDC began helping local business owners to repair or refresh their buildings with a combination of new windows, redone facades, fresh paint, wooden signage, ornamental light fixtures, and canvas awnings. The plan was for property owners to pick up half of the tab, with grants from the City of St. Paul and the Metropolitan Council filling in the rest. To date, more than 33 buildings have signed on to the program, with impressive results. One Payne Avenue business owner, Maureen Marinao of the Schwietz Saloon, reports that her building's $100,000 facelift (she put up $50,000) helped business jump by 20 to 25 percent within two months.

Using funds that came in part from the city and St. Paul-based Western Bank, the ESNDC also purchased three properties along Payne, including the historic G.A. Johnson Building, and has slated them for redevelopment. "An attractive commercial strip is one of the most significant assets in making sure your neighborhood is vital and stable," says ESNDC Executive Director Mike Anderson. "It establishes the identity of the Payne-Phalen Lake neighborhood."

Payne Avenue and the East Side are by no means the only areas of St. Paul to see improvements in the last few years, however. A few miles away, on the other side of downtown, the West Seventh/Fort Road neighborhood has been radically transformed, thanks in large part to the arrival of the millions of visitors who attend Minnesota Wild games and other events at the Xcel Energy Center each year. What was once a stretch of scruffy bars and low-key retail establishments along West Seventh now features 10 new or recently revamped restaurants and bars. The Capital City Partnership has worked to take advantage of the street's newfound status, sponsoring the Capital City Trolley, which allows Minnesota Wild ticket-holders to park and dine at establishments in the West Seventh area (and in other neighborhoods), leave their car in the restaurant's parking lot, and take the trolley to and from the Xcel arena.

The West Seventh area is only one of the communities that the

Partnership has worked with as part of an exhaustive neighborhood outreach program. In 1996, the organization purchased the Taste of Minnesota festival; it now pumps 25 percent of the event's proceeds into local neighborhoods. The funding has taken a variety of forms. A few examples: When the Riverview Economic Development Corp. needed cash for the production of a new tourist brochure highlighting St. Paul's West Side, the Partnership quickly came up with an $1,800 grant. When the Highland Business Association needed money to cover part of its holiday lighting program, the Partnership immediately supplied $5,000. In the last several years, it has helped organize and fund a fashion and dining show put on by the Grand Avenue Business Association and its members. The group has also helped in a variety of other ways, raising money for the installation of a new dome on the St. Paul Cathedral, paying for off-duty police to patrol community festivals, helping fund individual district precinct plans, and more.

University matters

At one time, University Avenue was the commercial thoroughfare of the Twin Cities, and the primary link between the downtowns of Minneapolis and St. Paul. But the construction in the 1960s of I-94 changed that. The highway sliced through University's St. Paul neighborhoods, wiping out the old Rondo community and quickly changing the character and condition of the street. Much of the area went downhill. Prostitutes roamed the streets at night. Crime was a serious problem, and pornography was big business. The Faust and Flick theaters and the Belmont Club were seedy adult entertainment establishments that added to the neighborhood's shady reputation.

Over the past decade, however, the streetscape has changed dramatically. The X-rated theaters closed and dozens of businesses opened, thanks in part to an influx of enterprising Southeast-Asian immigrants. "Asian development really saved the avenue," says Brian McMahon, executive director of University UNITED, a nonprofit organization devoted in part to fostering links between the city and local business. "The energy of the Asian businesses and the small businesses generally are very vital to this street."

But as McMahon is quick to add, Asian businesses are not the only new projects going in on the avenue. In the last several years, a number of high-profile projects have been completed along University—including the full-scale redevelopment of the old Montgomery Ward catalog warehouse and department store buildings between Pascal and Hamline Avenues in the Summit-University neighborhood. The dilapidated buildings were demolished in January 1996, and a Chicago developer transformed the site into Midway Marketplace, a 485,000-square-foot, powerhouse retail center that features a Cub Foods, a Kmart, Herberger's and Mervyn's department stores, a Border's bookstore, and numerous other businesses. The $45 million project brought new vitality to the area, and created a ripple effect along the avenue.

The development hasn't been all retail, however. In the summer of 2001, community members broke ground for a senior citizens housing development called The Episcopal Homes project at Fairview and University. According to McMahon, it is the first time in more than 50 years that housing has gone up on the avenue.

The city has been an active partner in these and other developments. It recently stepped in with a $300,000 matching grant and loan initiative funded by its Sales Tax Area Redevelopment (STAR) program. STAR grants and loans, which are funded by revenue from St. Paul's half-cent sales tax, must be matched, $1 to $1, with private resources. University UNITED administers the funds to business owners looking to make capital improvements such as new windows, doors, lighting, security systems, and landscaping projects.

In the fall of 2001, St. Paul took another bold step toward bringing University Avenue back to life. In early October, the city council voted to proceed with plans to create the Pan Asian

Village, a new development proposed for the corner of University and Dale Street (an intersection where the Summit-University and Thomas-Dale neighborhoods meet). Proponents of the $40 million project, which will feature retail and restaurant space, a Southeast Asian cultural center, a theater, and 50 units of senior housing, say it will bring 300 new jobs to the area, and stimulate economic development all along the avenue. As this chapter was being written, the city was working with the project's developers to negotiate a purchase agreement with the site's current owner, the Krauss-Anderson construction firm, and considering whether to provide the developers with a STAR grant.

While the Pan-Asian Village still has a few hurdles to clear, it does illustrate the city's commitment to the area. With new housing and millions in new investments and development in the works, the street is poised for a renaissance rivaled only by downtown and the Phalen Corridor. And, with the additional possibility of the much-debated light rail system down University Avenue, the area, which has already seen such tremendous growth, could regain some of its lost significance.

New life for downtown

When Norm Coleman took office in early 1994, downtown was arguably St. Paul's most economically distressed neighborhood. The downtown business district had absorbed a number of serious blows in recent years: mainstay businesses such as West Publishing had left town, retailers were struggling, and the city's most prominent redevelopment plan—an idea to promote its lineup of arts and cultural attractions—was off to a sluggish start. On top of it all, there was a fundamental lack of cohesiveness downtown; business and City Hall often failed to agree on key issues, and the relationship between the two was often quite chilly. In sum, downtown was groping for an identity and sorely in need of direction.

As one of their first moves, Coleman's development team began thinking of downtown in a new light—as a neighborhood.

They turned to Ken Greenberg of Greenberg Consultants Ltd., a Toronto-based architectural and urban design firm, who had recently completed a widely praised master plan for the University of Minnesota. Greenberg condensed St. Paul's situation: As was the case with many cities, St. Paul had evolved into a collection of distinct, single-use areas during the 20th century. Downtown was primarily a business district. Citizens typically commuted into downtown from residential areas, and then traveled somewhere else for entertainment and recreation. What's more, he saw that St. Paul had become further isolated from its surrounding communities by a ring of highways and heavy industry. St. Paul was walled off by I-94 and 35E to the north and west and by the river valley to the south.

Greenberg proposed that St. Paul embrace mixed-use urban villages—developments which combine, as their name suggests, a variety of uses within their confines. "Thanks in part to the new, post-industrial economy, many cities across the country and the world were transforming their single-purpose central business districts in favor of a new plan in which uses were not segregated and separated from each other," he explains. "In that type of plan, people actually live close by to where they work. Recreation, shopping, and culture all exist cheek-by-jowl, and there's a rediscovery of urbanity and the pleasures of city life."

During the 1980s and early 1990s, a number of such communities had sprung up around the country (including in the Twin Cities), either on their own or through municipal planning efforts. Across the river in Minneapolis, young professionals and empty-nesters were buying into several new residential developments on the fringes of that city's Warehouse District and along the Mississippi. St. Paul's own Grand Avenue had shed its old identity as a down-at-the-heels commercial strip and refashioned itself into a tony shopping and residential locale.

Even closer to home, the Lowertown area of downtown had its own mixed-use neighborhood, complete with warehouses-turned-condominiums, city-subsidized artist's lofts, the St. Paul

Farmer's Market, and a handful of restaurants, all within walking distance of Mears Park, a four-block-square urban greenspace.

In 1997, Coleman unveiled the "St. Paul on the Mississippi Development Framework," a plan that fundamentally reshaped the traditional urban model. A core element of that model, as Coleman explains, is the creation of an interconnected system of urban villages throughout and around downtown. "We are creating a city where people work, play, and live," he says. "These villages will help tie those elements together."

As 2001 drew to a close, that vision was taking shape. In addition to the proposed Pan-Asian village on University Avenue, a number of other villages were in various stages of progress, with more queued up in the development pipeline. One, the $80 million North Quadrant project, which is set to open in February 2002 on the northern fringes of downtown, will feature a combination of housing and retail. Another, the Upper Landing development, will create 600 units of rental and owner-occupied housing and 2,300 square feet of commercial and public open space on a former brownfield site along the Mississippi. Directly across the river from downtown, the West Side Flats Urban Village will feature more than 600 housing units and a U.S. Bancorp client service center. A few miles upriver, the River Bluff project will transform a heavily polluted former petroleum tank farm into yet another 600-unit residential development with an additional 80,000 square feet of commercial space.

The city has taken a number of other steps to make downtown look and feel more like the "big small town" that Coleman describes. In 1999, St. Paul kicked off a five-year effort to reconstruct downtown streets, repaving them with colored blocks, and adding planters and ornamental light fixtures. In 2000, it installed new observation decks and iron stairways on the Wabasha Street bridge, encouraging pedestrian traffic from downtown to Raspberry Island. And in the spring of 2001, the city completed a $14 million revitalization of Harriet Island Regional Park; the park now features new walking trails, boat docks, a Michael Gravesdesigned performance stage, and a pavilion for special events.

To be sure, the various city agencies involved in these and other projects deserve credit for their work. But they weren't the only parties involved in the effort. For one, investment from individuals and companies has helped fuel many of the city's improvements—the Harriet Island project alone featured approximately $5 million in private contributions. And as the various neighborhood projects illustrate, progress really starts to happen in St. Paul when the public and private sector work together.

Given the intense pace of city redevelopment during the Coleman Administration, it would be impossible to lay out all of the projects that have gotten underway in St. Paul's neighborhoods over the last half-decade or so. Nonetheless, examples such as the work being done in the Phalen Corridor, along Payne and University Avenues, and elsewhere do help illustrate how the city and a broad assemblage of organizations have worked together. By themselves, specific neighborhood examples offer case studies on how to jump-start and bolster community development. Add them together, however, and they offer something else, and something far more powerful: a way to create a larger, cohesive neighborhood—the "integrated urban mesh" that Coleman refers to.

City Living

St. Paul is now gearing up for the next stage in its revival: the creation of a permanent base of downtown residents.

BY MARY LAHR SCHIER

Betty Herbert lives downtown, loves downtown, sells downtown. A real estate agent with a shock of silver hair and a gregarious personality, Herbert has seen downtown St. Paul at its highest and lowest points. She bought her first condominium in the City Walk building on East Ninth Street in St. Paul before builders broke ground. It was the early 1980s, the country was struggling to pull out of a recession, and interest rates on home mortgages flirted with 15 percent. Herbert had raised her family in Marine-on-St. Croix. Though she'd never lived in the city before, she decided that with her children grown, she wanted a livelier, more urban environment. The condos at City Walk seemed perfect. She loved the views, the skyway connections to downtown shopping or entertainment, and getting rid of her lawnmower and snow shovels. Even better, because the condos were financed in part by the St. Paul Port Authority, Herbert and her neighbors were eligible for mortgages at the then-shockingly low rate of $9^{3/4}$ percent. "I figured there's no way I could lose," she recalls.

But as she discovered, "Minnesotans take a little longer to catch on to new ideas. The general thinking was, 'Don't buy a condo, you'll never be able to sell it,'" she notes. For awhile, that proved true. The economy did not recover quickly and condos at Galtier Plaza in Lowertown came on the market at about the same time as those at City Walk. Then, the Pointe of St. Paul was built in 1988, producing a glut of high-rise units. In the late 1980s, as interests rates dropped, Herbert and her neighbors tried to refinance. Many could not because bankers valued the units at less than the mortgages. In the early 1990s, things hit bottom. Downtown St. Paul was dragging and a one-bedroom unit at City Walk with an underground garage stall sold for only $40,000, about two-thirds of its original market value.

What a difference a few years—and a different attitude in the city—make. By 2001, units in City Walk sold for close to $100,000, and plans for hundreds of new townhouses and condos in the downtown core were under construction or in the planning stages. Some buildings were close to selling out before construction began. The boom in housing grew from several changes in St. Paul and its population: demographics that favor downtown living, a more attractive downtown to live in, and increasing demand for housing of all kinds.

"The next phase of downtown development is all about housing," says Brian Sweeney, director of St. Paul's Planning & Economic Development department. The reasons for the focus on housing are plentiful. First, people who live downtown spend four times more than a person who works there does. They also care much more about safety, amenities, and the quality of life in the downtown core. "What housing creates is another kind of stakeholder," says Patrick Seeb, executive director of the St. Paul Riverfront Corp., which has been involved in the planning of two of the major housing projects in the city. "Everyone who owns a condo or townhouse in downtown becomes a stakeholder. They also add a dynamism to downtown that isn't there with someone who works or just visits downtown. They're there at night. They're walking the streets. They're part of the life of the city."

Housing in downtown has always been a part of the Capital City Partnership's plan for improving the city. Mayor Norm Coleman began pushing housing as a segment of downtown and riverfront development from his first days in office. "When people are around on the streets, the streets are safer. They're our streets," he told a reporter from *Mpls/St. Paul* magazine in 1995. But to create that housing, Coleman needed a more lively economy and a plan which would produce housing that responded to market desires. So as the city worked to build employment and commercial property values downtown, it also pursued plans that would provide marketable downtown housing for the future.

It takes a village

In 1994, urban planner Ken Greenberg of Greenberg Consultants Ltd., a Toronto-based architectural firm, was working with the University of Minnesota to create a master plan for the school's campus. Coleman dispatched a group from his economic development team to get Greenberg's thoughts about working around the riverfront. Greenberg, knew about St. Paul native Benjamin Thompson's drawing of the Great River Park, an imagining of what St. Paul could look like with a greener, more park-like riverfront. Other architects and urban planners from the university had fleshed out that drawing more, but Coleman and city officials felt more detail and more community involvement would accelerate revitalization of the riverfront and downtown core. With financial backing from the Capital City Partnership and the St. Paul Riverfront Corp., the city retained Greenberg to guide the city's planning process. "When this all started, it was clear that no one had a monopoly on answers or the right approach. A lot of knowledge had to be drawn out quickly," says Greenberg. That's when the city began holding "charettes," a series of town meetings designed to draw out community opinions about the relationship between the city and the river. A wide range of people would be brought together for a day. They would talk about the city and its problems and its hopes and what it needed. They talked about the river and how it could be the focus of the city's future. Then the participants got out pencils and maps and started drawing the city of their imagination.

From these meetings came the "St. Paul on the Mississippi Development Framework," a collection of drawings, design guidelines, and development principles that would govern how the city approached development in the crescent that runs from the State Capitol through downtown and around the Mississippi River. The plan envisioned a "system of interconnected, mixed-use urban villages, nestled in the lush green of a reforested river valley." Each village would radiate from around a central park and would include places to live as well as places to work. They would be neighborhoods, not just commercial districts. The idea of urban villages had been around since the 1960s—though ignored almost completely by most city planners bent on segregating where people lived from where they worked or shopped. In her landmark book, *The Death and Life of Great American Cities*, author Jane Jacobs called for urban environments that encouraged a mix of housing, commercial, and retail spaces; public parks; and pedestrian-friendly streets that invited people to connect with each other and the environment. "No single element in a city is, in truth, the kingpin or the key," says Jacobs. "The mixture itself is kingpin, and its mutual support is the order."

St. Paul already had seen the potential of a mixed-use urban village. Beginning in 1978, with a $10 million grant from the McKnight Foundation, the Lowertown Redevelopment Corp. had been fashioning an urban village among the old warehouses and abandoned buildings of Lowertown. Mears Park, with its shaded benches and open green lawn, crossed by sidewalks and a gentle brook, sits like an oasis amidst the neighborhood. The park provides a gathering point for a wide range of workers, residents and visitors to the area. Twenty years after its inception, despite some struggles, Lowertown is now home to dozens of businesses (including many high-tech firms), the successful St. Paul Farmer's Market, a vibrant artist's community, and more than 1,500 lofts and condos in a variety of price ranges. Most of Lowertown's housing—like a lot of the city's efforts in the 1980s and early 1990s—has been rehabbed, often out of old warehouses. "Since the late 1980s, the policy of the city had been not to build new units, but to rehab old ones," says Sweeney. That decision was part policy, part practicality.

Obstacles to creating new urban villages, such as those outlined in the city's development framework, ranged from dealing with recalcitrant property owners to pollution problems associated with old industrial sites. "There wasn't a single piece of property available for development near downtown that didn't have a pollution issue," says Sweeney, speaking of the industrial past of many of the most likely housing sites. Moreover, the city needed to create the right environment to attract residents before any housing plan could be successful. It needed first to build its commercial base, develop the cultural amenities that make living in downtown exciting and wait until a market for housing emerged. By the year 2000, that time had arrived.

The collision of demographics and opportunity

It's a cold Saturday in September 2001. Despite a steady downpour, a parade of visitors tiptoe around deep, muddy puddles to get a glimpse of Essex on the Park, the first phase of St. Paul's North Quadrant housing development. The North Quadrant was one of nine new urban villages proposed in the city's development framework in 1997. It is an area that had seen every aspect of urban life. It had once been a neighborhood known for its fashionable residences—James J. Hill lived at the corner of Wacouta and Eighth Streets. Then, it gradually evolved into a commercial area, and into then more of a warehouse district. In the 1980s, investors abandoned the area's aging structures. Many were bulldozed and turned into surface parking lots. The North Quadrant became a place to park, not live. With the opening of the Essex, a townhouse and condominium development, and its partner apartment building, the Sibley Park Apartments, in 2002, the area has come full circle.

The lookers at the Essex this rainy Saturday are mostly couples; some look young and prosperous: men with small, dark-framed glasses and women in black leather jackets and snug jeans. Others are older, a little grayer on top, a little fuller through the middle. They take off their shoes at the doorway of a model unit and trace the wood grain in the maple floor with their toes and run their hands reverently over the Corian countertops in the kitchen. You could have a great party at this house. Across the street is Wacouta Commons. The two-acre square is covered with mud, but soon will become a village green, and the center of neighborhood activities. Around the side of the block, where West Seventh Street curves, plans call for a new, 10,000-square-foot retail area. The lower level of the Sibley Park Apartments, next to Essex on the Park, will house shops, such as restaurants, a grocery or deli, a dry cleaner or coffee shop. Despite the area's past as a fringe neighborhood of downtown, visitors can feel that this will be an exciting place to live soon. Thirty of the 38 units in the Essex were sold months before building completion. The apartments at Sibley Park also are expected to be completely re-served prior to completion of construction.

The visitors to the Essex model are exactly the people the city expects will drive future housing development in downtown. "Mostly we're looking at old Baby Boomers and young couples who are doing far too well financially," says Sweeney. Local real estate agents divide likely downtown buyers into four general categories. Many are young professionals, singles or couples, with good jobs, most likely in downtown. Another group is older, what one real estate agent calls "recovering ex-hippies who want to move downtown to relive the experiences of their youth." These older residents tend to be in their 50s, seeking a way to move into an active retirement. The third group includes many same-sex couples, also usually professionals, who find greater acceptance in downtown and often respond well to the historical buildings in the area. The final group includes those who fit no category at all but love the city.

"For a lot of people, if they look at the option of buying a three-bedroom rambler in Richfield for $250,000 or spending the same amount of money on a really nice condominium in downtown, downtown looks pretty good," says Jay Nord, an agent who is representing developers of the Great Northern Lofts, an abandoned commercial building being rehabbed into 52 condos in Lowertown.

"We weren't targeting a demographic—we were creating an attractive housing opportunity," says Coleman. "I think urban living is, by nature, attractive to Baby Boomers, folks who don't want to worry about shoveling the snow and mowing the lawn. I can't tell you about the new generation, but if there's enough entertainment, if there's vitality, it will appeal to them, too.

In 1999, the city, the Capital City Partnership, and the St. Paul Riverfront Corp. commissioned a study of potential housing demand in downtown between the years 2000 and 2010. The study found that demand for downtown housing would be strong enough to merit the development of between 1,400 and 1,900 new housing units during the 10-year span. Increased downtown employment, an improved cultural environment downtown, and an overall tight housing market for the Twin Cities would all contribute to the need for more housing, the study noted.

As for solutions, the study recommended condominium units similar to those at the Essex on the Park, and its companion building the Dakota on the Park, which will be built in 2002. Both buildings are four stories tall, with two-story townhouses on the lowest level and two floors of apartment-style flats up above. Architecturally, they resemble the older structures in the neighborhood, with front stoops, a brick exterior and architecturally interesting features at the top. Developed by George Sherman and Associates and the Michael Lander Group, the $45 million project eventually will include 75 condominiums and townhouses and 225 apartments. The Essex townhouses and condominiums are priced between $125,000 and $350,000. Units at the Dakota will run from $159,000 to $450,000. While apartments in the North Quadrant may rent for up to $2,500 a month, 20 percent of the rental units will be priced to be affordable for families earning 50 percent of St. Paul's median income. In keeping with the city's affordable housing goals, another 10 percent will be priced for those at 30 percent of the city's median income.

Bringing housing back to the river

The North Quadrant development is the first of three major housing projects planned for the city in the next few years. In late 2001, work began to clean up pollution and increase soil levels for a large mixed-use development on the Upper Landing. Bounded by the High Bridge, the Mississippi River, Chestnut Street, and the newly revamped Shepard Road, the Upper Landing has had as checkered a past as the North Quadrant. Initially settled by squatters looking for quick access to the river and cheap land, the site served as St. Paul's Little Italy from the early 1900s to the 1960s. At one time, about 400 people lived in mostly owner-occupied houses near the river. However, the area flooded repeatedly, and serious floods in 1965 and 1969 convinced the city to offer a buyout to the Upper Landing's homeowners. Later, the city built a floodwall and the area became industrial. While its proximity to the river made the Upper Landing an attractive site for housing, its past required that the city and the developers remove tons of contaminated earth and raise the soil to levels reached only by a 500-year flood.

"Investments were happening all around it," says Pat Seeb of the St. Paul Riverfront Corp. "There was the Science Museum; Shepard Road was relocated; Harriet Island was improved." Then, Texas-based developer Centex approached the city about the Upper Landing and "was willing to spend a lot of money and a lot of time on the site," Seeb adds. The clean-up and soil improvement process will cost about $40 million, of which $3.7 million will be paid by state and Metropolitan Council grants and $6 million will be backed by a city loan. The remainder will be privately funded, with assistance through a 25-year tax-increment-financing district. The development overall is expected to cost about $120 million. Initial plans call for eight blocks of housing and other uses. Approximately 600 apartments, condos, and townhouses are planned, with construction beginning in 2002. The townhouses and condominiums will range in price from the low $200,000s to more than $500,000. About 20 percent of the apartments will be affordable units and Centex is working with Common Bond Communities, the Twin Cities' largest nonprofit housing provider, to build and manage those units.

The development also will capitalize on its riverside location. Housing closest to the river will include shorter buildings with taller ones built farther back to enhance and protect views of the river. A public trail is planned on the roadbed where the old Shepard Road used to run. The trail is expected to end at a plaza near Chestnut Street, and will include an overlook, possibly a park, and other public spaces. The city has asked Centex to develop the area in a way that reflects the rest of St. Paul, with streets that run perpendicular to each other and multiple road connections that link back to the city, especially to the entertainment options at the nearby Xcel Energy Arena and the Science Museum of Minnesota. The intention is that the development not feel like a "project" but like a neighborhood.

A second large urban village is in the planning stages for the area across the Mississippi River from downtown. The West Side Flats has a background similar to the Upper Landing region. For many years, it was home to ethnic communities, including Eastern European Jews and, most recently, Mexicans. Flooding problems also plagued those neighborhoods and gradually the 45-acre parcel shifted to more industrial uses. When those were abandoned, vacant land emerged, creating a barren gap between the river and the cozy West Side neighborhoods on the bluffs above.

The city's master plan for the area calls for a neighborhood that feels like one of St. Paul's older communities. It will contain a mix of office space, shops and restaurants, and rental and owner-occupied housing at several price levels. Throughout the neighborhood will be several parks, including a riverfront esplanade, a greenway connecting the river to Plato Avenue, and a neighborhood park. Streets laid out on a grid system will link the neighborhood to downtown and to the rest of the West Side.

The commercial centerpiece of the area will be a 150,000-square-foot office building for the operations center of U.S. Bancorp. The building will bring about 2,200 employees to the West Side in late 2002. A five-level parking ramp with space for 1,400 cars will be completed about the same time. U.S. Bank plans to add a second office building with about 200,000 square feet of space about a year later. The city will assist the company with the $79 million project by providing $15 million in tax-increment financing.

The project grew out of the involvement of U.S. Bank officials in the Capital City Partnership, says John W. Murphy, Minnesota state chairman of U.S. Bank and U.S. Bancorp. "Over the last several years, we have gotten very excited about the opportunities in St. Paul and the leadership Norm Coleman has brought to the process. He's like a horse—you give him a little rein and he runs harder," Murphy says. "We were going to build something anyway. The opportunity to have housing and retail nearby seemed extraordinary, especially right on the river. We could have built this a lot cheaper in another location, but this is just a better place to be."

U.S. Bank broke ground for the building in October 2001. The bank building will face Robert Street on the east edge of the development and will be perpendicular to the river, increasing the amount of public park-space along the river. While specifics on the remainder of the West Side Flats area have not been determined, the city's master plan for the area calls for about 1,000 housing units. Most of these will be rentals priced for moderate-income residents. The master plan describes courtyard apartments, rowhouses, and some old-fashioned "live-above-the-store" residences. About 250 units will be owner-occupied condominiums and brownstone-style townhouses with prices ranging from $200,000 on up. Most of the property slated for housing development is owned by JLT West Side LLC, and is being developed in association with Sherman and Associates, one of the developers on the North Quadrant project.

These new neighborhoods, says designer Greenberg, "will be picking up the flavor of older, successful neighborhoods." They are attractive places to live because of their proximity to the amenities of downtown and to the natural beauty of the river.

They also can be simple, pleasant places to live, says Betty Herbert, who finds she enjoys downtown living more each year, especially as traffic gets more congested. From her condominium in the City Walk building, Herbert watches the traffic on I-94 every morning and feels grateful not to be in it. "Living downtown is a pleasure," she says. "I walk to the Ordway; I walk to shopping or to do business. It's really a nice way to live."

Recreating Retail

Downtowns aren't the shopping "centers"
they used to be. St. Paul has responded in
some creative ways.

BY GENE REBECK

Look at a photograph of downtown St. Paul around, say, 1941, and two things that would strike you would be (1) how many people there are on the sidewalks, and (2) the abundance of stores, banks, theaters, and restaurants. In fact, you'd see such a density of business frontages that you might wonder: Were the city's blocks somehow bigger back then?

That density was something of an optical illusion, since the city's old zoning laws allowed storefronts to be less than 30 feet wide back then. But the fact remained that, as was true for other cities, downtown was St. Paul's main shopping center, where the city's energy and excitement were most concentrated, where all types of people came to shop, enjoy themselves, and enjoy each other. Its streets were a stage upon which all kinds of human dramas played out.

Back before World War II, the city boasted several major department stores: The Golden Rule, Field-Schlick, Schuneman's,

110

and The Emporium, to name four of the biggest. In these palaces of commerce, one could buy just about anything: clothing, model railroads, cathedral radios, old coins, musical instruments, hunting rifles, books, and records. These big stores were native to downtown St. Paul, just as stores like Powers, Donaldson's, and Dayton's were born in the city to the west. In addition to the big stores, there were numerous smaller shops in St. Paul—drugstores, jewelers, haberdashers, pet stores. Downtown also was where people came for stage performances and first-run movies, where the big banks had their headquarters, and where most of the city's finest restaurants were found.

The scenes in those photographs from just half a century back seem very far away. The postwar triumph of the private automobile over mass transit, the decline of the downtown residential base, the spread of the suburbs, the blossoming of malls, the rise of national-chain retailers and discounters such as Gap and Target, and the decline of the big department store in favor of big specialist chains all steadily eroded the retail dominance of urban downtowns. One by one, St. Paul's native department stores were either bought out or closed. By the late 1970s, all had vanished. The smaller boutiques and specialty stores also closed—names like Frank Murphy, Peck & Peck, and Liemandt's have disappeared, except in the memories of older St. Paulites.

To be sure, the city did fight back. Its chief weapon was taken from the suburbs' own arsenal—the enclosed shopped mall. In 1980, the city built Town Square across Cedar Avenue from the Dayton's store, anchored by a hotel and the now-defunct Minneapolis-based store, Donaldson's. But within 15 years, Donaldson's was closed and most of the smaller shops had also departed. Another indoor mall was opened on the first several floors of Galtier Plaza in Lowertown in 1986, but it didn't even have a big name to anchor it, and as a retail venue it was largely doomed from the start. A year later, the World Trade Center opened with great fanfare, with national chains Victoria's Secret and Eddie Bauer putting stores there. But within a few years, those two shops had disappeared. Only the center's food court, catering mostly to workers, was still prospering.

This kind of retail decline is by no means peculiar to St. Paul. Even Minneapolis, which is considered to have been highly successful in keeping its downtown retail base, has seen that base shrink over the past decade. Of that city's own department stores, only Dayton's remains, and even that has been rebranded with the name of a Chicago-born retailer, Marshall Field's, which Dayton's parent company—then Dayton Hudson, now Target Corp.—bought in 1990. Minneapolis also had developed several enclosed malls in its downtown, but these have not been much more successful than St. Paul's. St. Anthony Main, Butler Square, and the Conservatory have all ceased operations as retail centers. Those that remain, such as City Center and Gaviidae Common, have been facing struggles of their own, losing key tenants.

The failure of the malls to thrive reinforced in many people's minds in the mid-'90s notion that downtown St. Paul was moribund. To be sure, people were still working downtown—and so long as St. Paul is the state capital, they always would be. But rightly or wrongly, most measure the health of a downtown by the number and vibrancy of its stores and restaurants. The office buildings could all be full, but no one outside them sees that these buildings are successful. Offices would not bring anyone besides their occupants back to the city center. An after-hours retail life was essential to downtown's long-term health.

As Mayor Norm Coleman and other interested parties discussed how to stanch the retail bleeding in downtown St. Paul, they agreed that the me-too mall approach was not working. The reality had to be faced: Downtown St. Paul would never be the shopping center it was decades ago. That era was over, for good.

So what was to be done? Under the direction of Coleman and Capital City Partnership, St. Paul embarked on a different approach. In essence, it stood the old approach on its head. "If the city has made one consistent mistake in the last 20 years," says Brian Sweeney, head of St. Paul's Department of Planning &

Economic Development, "it has been trying to force retail." So instead of building gleaming new stores first and assuming, wrongly, that shoppers would naturally be lured to their lights like moths, you first built a critical mass of potential consumers. In the words of Partnership President and CEO John Labosky, "Retail follows traffic."

These consumers would inevitably shop differently than those who thronged to the Golden Rules and Emporiums of the first half of the last century. It might not be the case that many would be coming downtown primarily to shop and dine. Instead, they would be visiting the city center for some other purpose, and would then be drawn to spend money in stores or restaurants.

This meant making downtown more attractive as a visitor destination. It also entailed restoring the city center as a residential area.

Five steps to recovery

The approach the city and the Capital City Partnership created and put in action comprised five steps. The details of each have been discussed elsewhere in this book, but the overall plan discussed here shows how all these parts fit together into a coherent whole.

Step one was to maintain and then increase the number of office workers in the city core. The goal, very simply, was to increase the foot traffic in the city during the day. The city worked hard not only to keep important corporate citizens such as Ecolab and Minnesota Life headquartered downtown, but also to attract new tenants—most notably and spectacularly, Lawson Software. These efforts have paid off, increasing the number of people working in the city center from around 46,000 eight years ago to around 53,000 in 2001—a 15 percent upturn.

But however successful these efforts have been, they still can do nothing to break the concept of downtown St. Paul as a city that shuts down once the office workers have headed home. That's where the Partnership's step two comes in: Build arts and cultural venues.

To be sure, places like the Ordway and the Fitzgerald Theatre, as well as the Minnesota Museum of American Art and the Minnesota Children's Museum were already in place. But the base of attractions was still too small. What's more, these existing venues needed other places in order to build their own audiences to greater levels. And in perhaps its most notable success in this realm to date, the Partnership helped drive the development of a bigger, more spectacular Science Museum on Kellogg Boulevard, with a "back door" overlooking the Mississippi River and the bluffs beyond.

But the Mayor and the Partnership also understood an even wider selection of attractions were needed. Step three, then, involved the promotion and development of new entertainment venues. In this category belongs one of St. Paul's biggest successes, the conversion of the old Civic Center into RiverCentre, with the gleaming new Xcel Energy Center—home of the Minnesota Wild, the city's new NHL franchise.

Step four: housing. The Mayor and the Partnership and other city leaders saw that a key part of unburdening St. Paul from its image as a 9-to-5 city was to make the city center more residential. While some residential development (primarily in Lowertown, particularly in Galtier Plaza) occurred before the Partnership's founding, only about 2,500 people lived downtown at the end of the 1990s. With downtown living a national trend, notably among upscale empty-nesters, the time was right for St. Paul to increase its central residential base. And such development is in process, with an expected 2,500 units of new housing, covering a range of prices, due to be in place by 2006. From a retail perspective, this is important because, as Labosky notes, residents typically outspend visitors and office workers 4 to 1.

Finally, step five: the promotion of retail—stores and restaurants—in the downtown area. So far, this phase's early successes have been modest but encouraging. But it's unlikely they would have happened at all if the City of St. Paul hadn't been successful at a major retail effort—keeping its last downtown department store.

Saving Dayton's

If you worked downtown during the last 15 years, you often heard the rumors. Dayton's is going to close. Dayton's can't make any money there. They're staying open as a favor to the city, but they can't afford it for much longer. Throughout the 1980s and 1990s, many felt that if Dayton's were to go, downtown St. Paul would never be able to withstand the blow. There might still be some retailers and restaurants—the presence of the Capitol and its sizable workforce would guarantee that. But it would be a downtown filled with unsightly empty storefronts that would never be occupied.

Many felt there was a precedent for a Dayton's departure. Donaldson's came to St. Paul when it bought The Golden Rule in 1961. In 1980, it moved out of the grand old Golden Rule building on Seventh Street and became the anchor tenant in Town Square. By decade's end, however, Donaldson's had become a symbol of the tumultuous changes and rapid-fire consolidation in the "mainline" department-store industry. Chicago-based retailer Carson Pirie Scott snapped up the Donaldson's chain in 1988. The Donaldson's stores all became Carsons—for a while. Not long thereafter, Carsons was itself swallowed up by P. A. Bergner, a Milwaukee department-store chain. Then, in 1992, Bergner's declared bankruptcy, and shut down both the Town Square and the Minneapolis City Center Carsons in early 1993. The remaining seven Twin Cities Carsons were sold to Dayton Hudson two years later and converted to Mervyn's stores. (Only one Carson's store remains in Minnesota, at the Miracle Mile Shopping Center in Rochester.)

Carson's disappearance from Town Square left Dayton's as the only mainline department store remaining in downtown St. Paul. Built in 1963, its location—bounded by Sixth, Wabasha, and Cedar Streets—positions it squarely in the center of downtown's retail base. In addition, it currently accounts for about two-thirds of the city center's retail shopping space by itself. At 350,000 square feet, it has less than half of the retail square footage of Dayton's/Field's flagship in Minneapolis. Still, the St. Paul store is larger than most mall anchors: The Field's stores in the suburbs, with a couple of exceptions, are generally 260,000 square feet or less—comparable to other mall anchors. (The average Target, by the way, occupies 126,000 square feet.) But given modern-day retail realities, the St. Paul Dayton's was indeed too big and too inefficient.

Was it in danger of closing? In any case, city officials, led by Mayor Coleman, didn't wish to risk it. They saw saving the store as crucial to keeping the downtown revival on track. But they acknowledged that the store couldn't keep going as it was. Dayton's, however much it might want to keep its downtown St. Paul store open, was a business—and a publicly traded one at that, with responsibilities to shareholders.

The plan that emerged had two key elements. First, the store would be "right-sized" to a more efficient and profitable square footage of around 240,000. Second, to help facilitate the remodel, the city of St. Paul would contribute $6.5 million in the form of a forgivable loan. The city would "get the money back" over the next 10 years in tax levies on the property. Also written into the deal: If the store closed any time before the 10 years were up, Target Corp. would have to pay the loan back.

Though Target won't offer specifics on the final remodeling of the St. Paul Field's store (these plans are scheduled to be revealed in late 2001, according to Field's spokesperson Aimee Kane), it's likely that the furniture department on the fifth floor will be closed down, and that the men's "club" in the basement will be moved upstairs.

Rightsizing the Dayton's/Field's store was a key step in maintaining St. Paul as a retail destination. With the department-store industry consolidating and shrinking, it's unlikely another big store will come into town, Still, even as a smaller store, Field's symbolizes the seriousness of the city's commitment to retail development. It also shows to shoppers, current store-owners, and potential future retailers that the city is still alive as a retail destination. If Dayton's had left, notes Brian Sweeney, "it would have created a crisis in confidence" in downtown St. Paul.

Confidence and the Commons

Over the past few years, retail development in downtown St. Paul might still be considered cautious, but its confidence is steadily returning. The most notable expression of this confidence is Lawson Commons.

In terms of retail, Lawson Commons is, in a sense, two structures. One comprises the 21,720 square feet of retail space on the first floor of the office building facing St. Peter Street, which is owned by Frauenshuh Companies, which also owns the Lawson office structure. The other is the 18,000 square feet of retail on the first floor of the Lawson parking garage. This space, like the parking garage ramp, is owned by the city.

Lawson Commons first tried to lure big names like the Gap to its retail space, but had no luck. However, Lawson's St. Peter space has been able to fill its storefronts primarily with food retailers. National chains Chipotle Grill and Starbucks Coffee both have opened stores here. And Kincaid's, operated by Seattle-based Restaurants Unlimited (which also owns a Kincaid's in suburban Bloomington), has quickly become one of the most desirable dining venues in the city, popular with both power brokers and night-on-the-town couples.

But Kincaid's isn't by no means the only upscale dining option currently thriving in downtown St. Paul. That fact is remarkable in itself. Not so long ago, there were fine-dining places like Fitzgerald's in Galtier Plaza, Spazzo in the Union Depot, and L'etoile atop the St. Paul Hotel. All highly regarded, all unable to survive. Kincaid's, however, has become one of three top downtown restaurants, the others being the St. Paul Grill, a clubby spot on the first floor of the St. Paul Hotel; and Pazzaluna, an Italian trattoria located cater-corner from the hotel at Fifth and St. Peter Streets.

The St. Paul Grill and Pazzaluna are run by locally based Morrissey Hospitality, which also operates Wildside Catering for the RiverCentre complex. Company President Bill Morrissey had created the Grill in 1990 while managing the St. Paul Hotel. By the late 1990s, he realized there was an opportunity to open another venue. "We had the proven success of the Grill, which is in what we call the 'casual upscale' dining segment," Morrissey recalls. "And we had excessive demand. So we thought that the market was ready for another restaurant. We looked around this area and at the types of restaurants that were represented, and we saw that Italian was underserved."

Then there's the distinctive example of the combined Northwest Opticians and Dunn Brothers Coffee on the corner of Wabasha and Fifth, in the retail space fronting the Lawson Commons garage. Northwest Opticians, founded by current owner Roger Schultz's father, has been a fixture in downtown for over half a century. When Schultz was forced to move his store, he coveted a particular space at Lawson Commons. But he was told that a coffee shop was the preferred tenant for that location.

Conferring with his wife, Schultz hit upon on an innovative solution: Why not create a combined coffeehouse/eyewear retailer? He contacted Dunn's, a Twin Cities-based coffeehouse franchiser, which was open to such a curious marriage. The results have been as remarkable as the concept. "Our business is up substantially on the optical side," Schultz says. "A lot of it is due to the traffic the coffee shop creates," though he adds that "we also have a better location than where we were [before the shop moved]." Dunn Brothers, meanwhile, notes that the downtown franchise is one of its most popular.

Downtown's distinction

That kind of distinctiveness is what people seek from urban retailers. People want cities to be different from suburbs. Downtowns across the United States are making a comeback because they have romance. In a *Wall Street Journal* review of *Downtown: Its Rise and Fall 1880-1950*, a book by MIT professor Robert M. Fogelson published in October 2001, Christopher Caldwell observes that "The reigning Wal-Mart model of American planning has proven functional and freedom-enhancing, but no one ever felt a surge of drama and nobility as he turned into a shopping-mall parking lot." Only cities can offer this sense of excitement— if they are encouraged to be more than a functional location for office employees. Mayor Coleman, the Capital City Partnership, and their fellow visionaries understood that if downtown St. Paul were to truly flourish as a retail center, it also needed to offer an alluring experience—one that was energetic, intimate, and visually and humanly diverse. In a word, urbane. The vision was the downtown as a source of entertainment.

For some, treating a city as "entertainment" might seem hollow and offensive. But downtowns have traditionally provided spectacle, often by simply being a city's chief destination. Older people still remember a trip downtown when they were younger as a big event: Dressing up before taking a ride in the streetcar or bus; the morning spent in one of the great department stores, whose high ceilings and colorful displays were meant to dazzle and awe, especially at Christmastime; lunch at a busy restaurant amid the tintinnabulations of silverware and china and water glasses. Movie theaters and train stations were also designed to convey this sense of ceremonious pleasure.

We live in less formal times, when a term like "upscale casual" isn't an oxymoron. But downtown can still provide people a sense of playing a part in a human drama. Putting together all the elements that make downtown appealing and exciting—housing, entertainment, retail—was one of the key reasons why the Capital City Partnership was formed. Retail development couldn't happen in a vacuum. People had to be attracted to other aspects of a downtown besides shopping—after all, they could shop just about anywhere. But what enclosed mall could offer one-of-a-kind venues such as the Science Museum, the Ordway Center, or the Xcel Center during hockey season? What suburb could offer the pleasures of walking across a Wabasha Bridge, with its elegant light poles and high span over the great river?

What the mayor, the Partnership, and their allies have grasped is that in the modern urban downtown, entertainment (however it's defined) and retail are intertwined. A family coming into downtown St. Paul to spend a Saturday morning at the Children's Museum, for instance, will want to stop somewhere for lunch—most likely, some place more interesting and leisurely than a food court favored by an on-the-go office worker.

Drama demands variety, and the unexpected. It's unlikely (though not impossible) that familiar names Old Navy and Barnes & Noble will be lured into downtown St. Paul. Instead, the city's vision for downtown comprises street-level, mostly home-grown shops that arise organically from the needs of visitors (and residents) and the creativity of retail entrepreneurs. Unlike a mall, such an approach would allow for the unpredictable and surprising—think of the Northwest Opticians/Dunn Brothers union, for instance.

For downtown St. Paul, the model here is very close to home—inside the city limits, in fact. Just to the west, Grand Avenue has become one of the Twin Cities' most desirable and envied retail districts, with mostly one-of-a-kind stores, along with a few national chains, such as Smith & Hawken and Restoration Hardware. And outside of the Victoria Crossing development, most of the stores on Grand Avenue have outside entrances.

As envisioned by Mayor Coleman and the Capital City Partnership, new downtown shopping would be focused on two retail "spines" running through downtown: the parallel streets of Wabasha and St. Peter. The focal points would be the Field's store on Wabasha and Sixth, spreading out along the Seventh Place Mall, the currently unused Wabasha Court block, and the retail area (owned by the St. Paul Port Authority) built into the first floor of the Lawson Commons parking garage.

The vision took a big step forward in early October 2001, when David Frauenshuh, the prominent downtown-property owner who helped lead the efforts to bring Lawson Software to St. Paul, purchased the blighted Wabasha Court property for $2.5 million. The current building will be razed, and the land will serve temporarily as surface parking until Frauenshuh and the city can negotiate the building of a larger structure, which as of this writing is expected to include office space and first-floor retail.

Note: first-floor retail. In a sense, this idea flies in the face of a long-time phenomenon in the downtowns of both Twin Cities. The skyway systems were considered great boosts for the downtowns when they began to be built in the 1960s. Working on the not-unreasonable notion that the advantage of suburban malls was their enclosure from the elements, the cities decided that they would, in effect, turn their downtowns into malls. Minneapolis even renamed its main shopping street Nicollet Mall, and closed it to regular car traffic. In the mid-1980s, the city even considered enclosing several blocks of Nicollet with a clear dome.

Three decades later, the skyways' legacy has to be considered something of a mixed blessing. On one hand, their convenience has been a big help to maintaining and building office occupancy: Busy workers don't need to put on coats and hats when rushing off to lunch or errands. On the other, they have helped drain downtown streets of life and commerce—which, in a urban downtown, go hand in hand. The effect has been far more pronounced in St. Paul, where numerous older, street-friendly structures have given way to buildings that are closed in on themselves, with retail operations—mostly convenience stores and food courts—clustering at certain "nodes" in the skyway system.

Mayor Coleman and the Capital City Partnership have understood that people crave the vibrancy that only an urban center can provide. And this sense of energy means street life and outdoor activity.

"The anomaly is that when you look at places like Grand Avenue, which are not even downtown, which don't have skyways but have the same climate, they have a lively retail life," says Ken Greenberg, a Toronto-based urban planner and architect who has consulted with the city on downtown development. "So one of the things that we promoted that has actually started to happen, for example, on St. Peter, is to get some of the retail and hospitality—the restaurants and bars and clubs and so forth—back down on the street level, where they can actually function evenings and weekends, and relate to, for example, the activities around Rice Park."

In this context, it's worth mentioning a very special kind of downtown retail activity: the St. Paul Farmers' Market. Located in Lowertown at Fifth and Wall Streets, this open-air market is distinctive from a great many others of its kind in that the produce sold there is all grown in the area. (Minneapolis's' market has no such requirement.) Though the St. Paul Farmers' Market has a 150-year history, it has been in its current location about 15 years, and city leaders believe it has needed a rehab for some time.

And it's getting one. The market's redesign and reconfiguration, scheduled for completion in 2004, will include the construction of a new indoor hall adjacent to the open-air market. "The indoor market hall will be a place where farmers and ranchers from the entire state can possibly sell their products," says Patrick Seeb, executive director of the St. Paul Riverfront Corp., whose Design Center is providing assistance on the market redesign. "The meat locker in New Ulm, for example, that has a certain kind of meat that is unique—a Bavarian style of beef, perhaps—or the apple orchard in Red Wing with a certain value-added apple product, could then sell their products there so that small farmers in Minnesota have an outlet for their products in this marketplace." The hall will be built on the market's current parking area, with an underground parking lot built to replace it.

Over the next three to five years, the city is envisioning the emergence of smaller retail venues "that benefit from the kind of traffic flow and people activity," in the words of Seeb. "In the river valley area, we are going to start to see activity-oriented retail like places that sell bicycles and outdoor clothing and gear and canoes and kayaks. I think we'll see retail that reflects the character of the neighborhood."

The city's intention has not been to serve as a retail developer, working to attract specific retailers to the city center. That is the market's job, and the failure of the indoor malls points to how precarious such an approach is. Instead, Mayor Coleman and the Capital City Partnership have sought to create an environment that potential retailers would find attractive.

The results, so far, have been modest but encouraging. The most notable new forms of retail have been focused around Lawson Commons. But the development of new eateries and watering holes down Seventh Street (such as the Downtowner Woodfire Grill, a former diner updated to appeal to an evening clientele, and Glockenspiel, a German restaurant in a former Czechoslovak social hall) in the direction of the Landmark Brewery also must be considered the results of the Partnership's downtown strategy, even if many of these places, strictly speaking, don't fall within downtown's four square miles. Still, the concertgoers and hockey fans thronging the Xcel Energy Center have no doubt driven much of this development.

Back to the streets

These days, many suburbs are trying to create a sense of urbanity themselves. Across the country, the enclosed-mall concept has grown a bit stale for many consumers, and suburbs are responding either by refurbishing their own downtowns or, in effect, creating downtowns from scratch. For instance, the Chicago suburb of Schaumburg—home to Woodfield, one of America's largest malls—pursued the latter course in early 1990s. Also in Schaumburg is a retail center designed to look like an city shopping district. It's called Streets of Woodfield.

From a retail perspective, downtown St. Paul can never return to its heyday more than half a century ago. No American downtown can. The retail market has changed, and so has the way people use their downtowns. Envisioning new kinds of retail for a new type of downtown has been a great challenge for St. Paul, and the process is ongoing. But time appears to be on its side. After several decades of suburban ascendancy, people realize how important urban centers are to them as places to gather, shop, play, and live. The energies and vision of Norm Coleman and the Capital City Partnership have taken advantage of a cultural moment. They may be even be helping to drive it.

The City Goes to Market

For Norm Coleman and the Capital City Partnership, rebuilding St. Paul went hand in hand with attracting new residents and visitors.

BY ANDREW BACSKAI

On an idyllic early-autumn evening, as a near-full moon reflects brightly off the still surface of the Mississippi River, people by the tens of thousands funnel into downtown St. Paul's new crown jewel, the Xcel Energy Center. Perched on the corner of Kellogg Boulevard and West Seventh Street, the gleaming arena opened nearly one year ago to the day—Oct. 10, 2000—to house the city's new NHL team, the Minnesota Wild, and to host the kinds of large-scale special events and musical concerts that previously lured capacity crowds across the river to Target Center.

Tonight's masses are outfitted in hunter green and cedar red—the colors of their beloved Wild. Their collective mood is upbeat. Many have just satisfied their culinary cravings at some of down-town's new upscale eateries, including Pazzaluna and Kincaid's. Others will indulge in post-game spirits and snacks at one of the 10 new bars and restaurants that have sprouted from the neigh-boring stretch of West Seventh since Xcel opened. All arrived via city streets that crisscross an urban landscape populated by elegantly understated new commercial buildings, dramatic new cultural venues, inviting coffee shops and retail outlets, and pampered parks and public art-bearing green spaces.

The atmosphere is electric. It's exactly the kind of environment city planners and promoters dreamed of nearly six years ago when Mayor Norm Coleman assembled the Capital City Partnership to reinforce St. Paul's sagging investor base, rebuild its commercial and cultural infrastructure, and reinvent the city's brand.

Enticing investors

By 1995, downtown St. Paul's across-the-board slump was anything but a well-kept secret. Major commercial tenants like West Publishing had systematically evacuated the city, and suitable successors had not stepped in to repopulate the labor pool. Plunging property values were encouraging homebuyers to shop for new digs elsewhere. And a strategy aimed at marketing the city's cultural offerings as a "Cultural Corridor" had not stimulated the growth and development of complementary destinations—restaurants, coffee shops, retail outlets, and the like. Consequently, downtown St. Paul didn't offer the kinds of enticing attractions to encourage visitors to extend outings to, say, the Minnesota Children's Museum, the Science Museum of Minnesota, or the Ordway.

In short, "St. Paul had been on a downward spiral," says Lee Koch, the Capital City Partnership's vice president and director of marketing. "The city had some real serious image problems; St. Paul's brand was not strong."

Koch and her Partnership colleagues were charged with the formidable task of overturning St. Paul's less-than-stellar public image. Problem was, the city they inherited had few marketable consumer offerings. The Partnership would have to devise an alternate strategy.

The first step was to identify the source of downtown's ailing economy and subsequent identity crisis. The Partnership's investigation, Koch says, closed in on two primary problem spots. First, St. Paul desperately lacked the kind of corporate and investor base necessary to ignite and then sustain urban renewal. "We just didn't have enough people whose future prosperity depended on the future prosperity of the city," she notes. "There simply weren't enough stakeholders."

Second, downtown's commercial, residential and cultural institutions were not working together with city government on a common development and marketing agenda. Instead, says Koch, "everyone was working on their own plans. There was no single vision, and absolutely no sense of teamwork."

The Partnership acted quickly on its findings. It assembled a 21-member coalition of downtown marketers. The group (which now has more than 50 members) featured representatives from the Ordway, the Minnesota History Center, and other cultural institutions; from such corporations as The St. Paul Companies, 3M, and Minnesota Life; members of the Building Owners and Managers Association; as well as city officials and St. Paul Riverfront Corp. staffers. Together they formulated an aggressive five-year marketing plan designed to mirror and support the city's five-year development plan, which has been written about elsewhere in this book.

"What we had to work with was a five-year economic development plan laid out by Norm Coleman which, at its base, had a vision for what the city would look and feel like at the end of those five years," Koch says. "Our job then, was to support that agenda as it moved along in its timetable. We needed to enhance the city's brand by communicating that message in meaningful ways, over and over again."

To start, Coleman and city officials worked to find willing downtown investors. Their "wish list" included businesses and corporations actively seeking commercial space for new corporate headquarters, as well as "at-risk" companies considering joining the exodus out of the city's 90-block core. Of course, re-

cent history was working against the courtship efforts of city officials. Over much of the past decade, Twin Cities business owners
and residents had been presented with a succession of well-artic-
ulated economic development and cultural revitalization plans
for St. Paul, only to watch the city continue to regress economically. Consequently, impassioned speeches and two-dimensional
artists' renderings wouldn't do this time. City planners could no
longer tell prospective investors about the future. They had to
show the future to them.

Lawson Software provided an ideal test case. The fast-growing
Lawson, a Minneapolis-based enterprise software company with
1,000 employees, would offer a solid foundation on which to
build the city's corporate investment structure. But as Koch
notes, St. Paul knew it had to approach Lawson in the right way.
"You can't just show up in the office of Bill Lawson [Lawson
Software's then-CEO] with a 200-page planning document," she
says. "What you have to have is a dynamic mayor who has a vision for his city, who already has new stakeholders and investors,
and who has a cadre behind him. And you need to be able to
more effectively demonstrate to people what you're doing and
convince them that it's actually happening. They need to see that
there's a renaissance happening in St. Paul and that they can be
in at the very beginning."

To that end, city promoters, armed with Quicktime software,
developed a customized virtual-reality presentation for Lawson
and his brother and business partner, Richard Lawson, that
demonstrated how their new headquarters might fit in to the
new-look downtown Coleman envisioned. In the navigable, "be-
fore-and-after-style" presentation, programmers hired by the
coalition created a three-dimensional likeness of Rice Park set
against the backdrop of the dilapidated Garrick parking ramp.
Then, they removed the ramp and the block's primarily undesir-
able retail tenants, and replaced them with a new Lawson Software building, offering views of the structure from the outside in
and from the inside out.

After the presentation, Coleman and Capital City President and CEO John Labosky embarked on a bit of low-tech campaigning. They visited Lawson's Minneapolis offices and shook hands with every employee they encountered on their tour. With the three-dimensional image of Lawson's new downtown headquarters etched in their minds, and having witnessed firsthand Coleman's commitment to the firm, the Lawsons were as confident as they could be in their decision to set up shop in downtown St. Paul. The Lawson deal included an array of financial incentives from the city, including its offer to purchase and operate the parking garage attached to the Lawson building. By early 1999, construction on the $101 million, 13-story brick-and-stone Lawson Commons was underway.

Coleman and the Partnership also courted outsiders such as the Minnesota Business Academy with, among other incentives and tools, its virtual reality-enhanced vision of the city-to-be. The result: Minnesota Business and its 250 students moved into two of the buildings on 10th and Wabasha streets formerly inhabited by the Science Museum of Minnesota before its move to the Mississippi riverfront. The school expects to have nearly 450 students in downtown by 2003. Music Tech, another educational institution, also was persuaded to move its operations downtown from Minneapolis.

While they fortified the city's corporate investor base, Coleman and the Partnership also targeted companies in their own backyard and worked to convince them that St. Paul was on the verge of large-scale change. Minnesota Life, for example, had outgrown its existing Robert Street site and was carefully surveying the suburbs for space that could accommodate its burgeoning workforce, which was growing by 10 percent annually. The company eventually found that space—across the street from its existing headquarters. Minnesota Life recently moved into a new 13-story building on the corner of Robert and Sixth. In addition to office space, the 635,000-square foot facility also houses a daycare center and a number skyway-level retail shops.

Likewise, Coleman and company worked to shore up downtown's cultural community, which already featured such popular fixtures as the Minnesota Museum of American Art, the Minnesota History Center, the Ordway, Park Square Theatre, and the Minnesota Children's Museum. Another high-profile cultural institution, the Science Museum, had been planning a move out of downtown since 1992. In fact, the museum had zeroed in on a plot of land across the river from downtown on which to construct a new facility. The reason was simple, says Partnership consultant Dick Broeker: Studies had revealed that people didn't want to come downtown. Even so, by employing aggressive marketing and persuasive campaigning, and by developing a mutually beneficial financial package, Coleman and other coalition members convinced museum officials to build on the downtown side of the river and serve as a pillar in the city's rapidly evolving landscape. So far, their decision has paid impressive dividends: In the fiscal year that ended June 30, 2001, the Science Museum welcomed 925,000 visitors and served another 200,000 through educational outreach programs. Meanwhile, across Kellogg Boulevard, the Xcel Energy Center attracted 1.6 million visitors in its first year.

All told, in Coleman's two terms in office, downtown St. Paul would ultimately attract approximately $1.7 billion in new construction, 18,000 new jobs, a new convention center, and 1.5 million square feet of new office space. Though each new tenant's circumstances were unique, they all were persuaded to invest in downtown St. Paul, in part, by a common message communicating a unified strategy and vision.

"There weren't a lot of corporations chomping at the bit to move their headquarters to downtown St. Paul," Koch says. "They all had basically the same issues: Is St. Paul really worth the kind of investment you're asking us to make? And we had to tell them, 'Yes, it is, and here's why: We have a vision. We're rebuilding the city and this is the part we want you to play. We need you to invest in our urban core and it'll invest in you. And here's how it will work.'"

Residential resurgence

As businesses starting moving downtown, so too did residents. Over the next five to eight years, the city hopes to increase downtown housing by 2,500 units, which represents a projected 4,400 residents. In addition to encouraging private investments in housing—and in businesses whose workers may opt to live downtown—the coalition is supporting the three distinct urban village projects on riverfront land in and near downtown St. Paul.

The first, the North Quadrant, will eventually consist of 900 housing units, retail sites, and a new public park on eight to 10 blocks downtown. This village, created by Minneapolis developers Sherman Associates and the Michael Lander Group, is set for occupancy in February 2002. Another village, the 600-unit Upper Landing project will stretch for about 25 acres along the river between Chestnut Street and the High Bridge. The West Side Flats, to be located between Wabasha, Robert, and Plato streets, will offer 900 housing units. Both projects will feature bike and jogging trails, green spaces, and retail shops.

As Coleman and the Capital City Partnership steadily guided their development plan through its predetermined framework—which was designed to use commercial and cultural cultivation as a means to stimulate residential community—the marketing committee kept pace, supporting and conveying the key messages at each stage. "Any marketing plan, whether it's for a city or for something else, is meant to bolster the development plan," Koch says. "In order to do that, it has to mirror the timetable of the development plan. Because as you're trying to move forward, you've got to keep all your audiences saying, 'Yeah, that idea sounds like it could work—St. Paul is a good place for me to invest.' The marketing must reinforce that message every step of the way.

"From a marketing perspective, we had to do things creatively at the outset to entice the first few pieces we needed for the puzzle," she adds. "Since then, momentum has sort of taken over and we've been able to make a lot more things happen."

Indeed, some three years into the development plan, downtown St. Paul's physical makeover was well underway. During one stint, in fact, 16 construction cranes jutted upward into the city's skyline. For the city's marketing team, it was now time to steer its strategy away from investor marketing and focus its energy on communication. The group's communications efforts extended literally from the ground into cyberspace. While Lawson Commons was under construction, for example, the Partnership commissioned a series of posters depicting what the finished product would look like. The posters were suspended from the fences that wrapped the construction zone, while a series of flags was installed around the site. Their purpose: Draw attention to the work-in-progress and serve as constant reminders that downtown St. Paul was being transformed.

The Partnership also developed a Web site, *ilovesaintpaul.com*, to provide visitors with a detailed look at plans for the city, as well as a calendar of and details about community events. The site also enables those who want regular development updates to sign up for the Capital City Partnership's e-newsletter, *What's Not to Love?* In addition, the Web site is a powerful tool for communicating key messages to the employees of Partnership member companies. Consider Minnesota Life, which features a prominent link to *ilovesaintpaul.com* on its corporate intranet. Given that approximately 88 percent of the firm's 2,400-person downtown workforce logs on to the intranet at least once a day, the link offers a powerful way to publicize downtown events.

Thanks in part to such well-coordinated efforts, the momentum had begun to shift in downtown's favor, and the perceptions of millions of annual visitors—Wild enthusiasts, theater-goers, gallery crawlers, and urban diners—already had begun to change. St. Paul's house was finally in order. It was time to start inviting guests.

The happy host

In 2000, the Capital City Partnership and the City of St. Paul launched "Peanuts on Parade," a public art initiative designed to honor St. Paul native and Peanuts creator Charles M. Schultz and to raise funds for a new sculpture garden—featuring bronze likenesses of the entire "Peanuts Gang"—adjacent to Rice Park. Twin Cities artists were commissioned to create custom-designed, 5-foot-tall Snoopy statues, which were sponsored by local companies and institutions to the tune of $5,000. Partnership Chairman Al Schuman, president of Ecolab, sponsored the first Snoopy, aptly named "Joe Clean." More than 100 local executives and business owners followed suit.

In addition to fulfilling its fundraising function, "Peanuts on Parade" also proved to be a marketing masterstroke. More than 500,000 visitors converged on St. Paul to see the Snoopy statues, which were situated throughout the city—from downtown's parks to the entrance of a dentist's office on the far reaches of West Seventh Street. As visitors toured the city snapping photos of the larger-than-life beagles, they also began to discover the newly revitalized St. Paul streets.

The following summer, the Partnership and the city unleashed a sequel: "Charlie Brown Around Town." Though the program's lead character had changed, the plot remained the same—thousands of visitors from around the world toured St. Paul in search of more than 100 artistically enhanced polyurethane statues.

In addition to its wildly successful Peanuts programs—which likely will continue for years to come—the Capital City Partnership also has assembled a diverse lineup of festivals and special events designed to heighten the sense of community among those who live and work in St. Paul, and to entice visitors to experience a reborn river city. In 1996, the group purchased the Taste of Minnesota, the state's largest free outdoor festival. The event, which showcases the offerings of local eateries and the talents of local and national musicians, was inspired by a similar event held in Chicago, which was attended in the early 1980s by Taste of Minnesota cofounder Ron Maddox. The Minnesota adaptation of the Taste concept draws roughly 500,000 people to the Minnesota State Capitol grounds over the Fourth of July weekend. Soon, perhaps by 2003, the ever-expanding festival will relocate to the riverfront, drawing those celebratory masses deeper into the downtown core.

The Taste of Minnesota grosses more than $3 million a year, which Maddox says "more than pays" for the festival. The Capital City Partnership reinvests festival profits into a variety of downtown marketing and neighborhood support initiatives. For instance, the Capital Flower Program was established in 1999 to beautify downtown during the summer months. In the winter, visitors are beckoned downtown to view the holiday lights that festoon the streets, structures, and green spaces.

The Partnership has also purchased Capital New Year, a downtown New Year's Eve celebration designed to be a family-friendly alternative to the holiday celebrations staged elsewhere in the Twin Cities. Like other offerings in the Partnership's special event stable, Capital New Year thrives because it showcases the city's natural charms—namely, its small-scale intimacy and European-style quaintness.

By late 2001, many key elements of the city Coleman envisioned years earlier had materialized. As was the case on that electric, early-fall Wild evening, "you now feel this sense of vibrancy in the city. There's an atmosphere of a thriving urban core," Koch says. "I'm not saying we're there yet. But the renaissance has begun."

After so many failed attempts to rebuild and sell St. Paul, why does this effort finally seem to be working? Any analysis has to start with the mayor. Without question, Coleman's passion and energy have given the city the spark it had long needed. On top of that, however, it has also been the result of a shared vision for the city—one in which a variety of diverse public and private organizations have pulled together to focus on a common goal.

A Continuing Journey

In 2004, a grand river voyage will celebrate how far St. Paul has come and how much further it hopes to go.

BY GENE REBECK

In its promotional materials, the Capital City Partnership often uses the word "imagine." Partnership President and CEO John Labosky also puts it this way: "Never stop dreaming."

Of all of the visions the Capital City Partnership, Mayor Norm Coleman, and their development allies have conjured up, none are quite as appealing as the notion of reviving the St. Paul Union Depot as a working train station. The lordly classical structure was the chief gateway for travelers coming to St. Paul until 1971, when the decline in train ridership, with only two trains passing through town, made the grand station seem outdated and impractical. Amtrak moved the station to a nondescript, utilitarian structure in the Midway area serving both St. Paul and Minneapolis.

These days, the Union Depot houses a couple of restaurants and the occasional special event—a useful function, but a far, far cry from its glamorous past, when presidents, celebrities, and just plain folks strode through the Depot's dramatic marble hallways. The last Amtrak train serving Minnesota, the Empire Builder between Chicago and Seattle, still goes by the Depot as it snakes through the river valley around the Mississippi's bends, but its local stop is miles from the heart of St. Paul.

The city's vision is to not only to return the Amtrak stop to the Depot, but to have the grande dame also function as a station for a light-rail line to downtown Minneapolis, which could then allow visitors by rail to connect to the airport and the Mall of America (and, of course, vice versa). The Depot thus would become not only the gateway to St. Paul, but the entire Twin Cities metropolitan area. Amtrak is enthusiastically supporting the idea of returning to the Depot, particularly in view of its plans to renovate the track between Chicago and the Twin Cities to accommodate high-speed trains.

It's an attractive vision, but the logistics involved mean that it will take some time to become real. In the meantime, something both visionary and very real is coming together in central St. Paul, on both sides of the Mississippi River.

The Grand Excursion

If you were able to walk over the tracks in back of the Depot, across Warner Road, and down to the river's edge, you'd find yourself at the approximate spot where, in 1854, seven steamboats carrying former President Millard Fillmore along with a number of statesmen, historians, poets, and East Coast newspapermen landed after chugging up the Mississippi from Rock Island, Ill., the terminus of a new "transcontinental" rail line from Chicago, and thus a link from the East to what was then the edge of the American frontier. The passengers landed with great fanfare and the city of St. Paul, then with a population of around 4,000, held a large festival with parties and fireworks.

That journey from the East to St. Paul was organized to promote the development of the upper Mississippi River valley. For St. Paul, then the territorial capital of Minnesota, it indeed had that effect. Newspaper reports of St. Paul and Minnesota, reaching readers back East, did much to lure new settlers to the area. "It led to some 30,000 people moving to Minnesota over the next few years," says Patrick Seeb, executive director of the Riverfront Corp. "It advanced statehood in Minnesota by probably a decade. And it really forever changed the destiny of this region."

Now a new Grand Excursion is being planned for 2004, the 150th anniversary of the original event. Spearheaded by the St. Paul Riverfront Corp., the new journey will recreate the trek from Rock Island to St. Paul, dramatizing the efforts St. Paul and various sister cities along the Mississippi have made to reconnect their identities with the great river. So far, the Riverfront Corp. has gotten some 35 cities to sign on.

While the specific events of the Grand Excursion 2004 are still being planned, the event is being framed by three major components—what the St. Paul Riverfront Corp., the mayor, the Capital City Partnership, and their allies term "commemorate, educate, and celebrate."

The commemorative element "involves telling the story of the reinvestment that has occurred, how this region has reclaimed its relationship with the Mississippi," says Seeb. That story will be told through a series of permanent bronze markers called the Mississippi Discovery Trail, from the Quad Cities to the Twin Cities, which will also recount the tale of the 1854 Grand Excursion. The education component, designed to teach people about the Mississippi and the river cities' relationship with it, will comprise a Web site, a Ken Burns-style documentary, and something called the "Exploration Trunk"—educational materials "stored" inside an old-fashioned storage trunk that will made available to schools along the Quad Cities-Twin Cities stretch of the river.

The final element is the celebration component. The signature event here is the "Grand Flotilla," which will leave the Quad Cities on the weekend of June 25, 2004. The flotilla will consist of about 12 to 15 paddleboats and steamboats ("the largest collection of passenger vessels and paddlewheel boats in recent history," Seeb says). Along the way, the boats will make stops at various river towns, with celebrations and events at each port of call. The flotilla will arrive in St. Paul on the Fourth of July weekend. There, a grand landing in downtown will culminate in more festivities and events (including the annual Taste of Minnesota, which will move from the Capitol grounds to the riverfront in 2003), when "all eyes will be on America's holiday on America's river," Seeb says.

The idea for retracing the Excursion originated in discussions Mayor Coleman conducted with other city leaders several years into his administration. There was a need, the mayor believed, to place St. Paul's redevelopment into a thematic timeframe. "If you're going to commit to this kind of urban revitalization, you know it can't be done over a year or two years," Seeb notes. "And you have to help people understand that. There will be good years and slower years, but you have to stay with it. You have to keep pounding away at it. Really, it's a 20-year investment."

But how do you keep up the energy level and commitment over such a long period of time? The mayor and the other leaders decided to frame this redevelopment effort over 10 years. After all, Coleman would not be mayor forever, and most of the rejuvenation and redevelopment efforts he inspired would have to be carried on by the community. And so a 10-year time horizon was created. Mayor Coleman having started the ball rolling in 1994, that meant 2004. When Mark Vander Schaaf, research coordinator for the city's Department of Planning & Economic Development, got wind of the idea, he wrote a letter to the mayor: "I understand you're aiming this redevelopment horizon for 2004. I want to tell you about this watershed event that occurred in 1854. Perhaps there's a way of linking the two." The new Great Excursion was underway.

The intention of the Grand Excursion is similar to that of the big landing 150 years earlier: to draw national and even international attention to St. Paul and the Mississippi River to showcase, in effect, the spirit of St. Paul. And in 2004, the city will have much to show.

Interplay

Above all, what it will show is a paradigm of interaction between the city's various elements. "Urban health really lies in the overlap between the economy, the community, and the environment," Seeb says. "We did as well as anybody in this country of separating the three. So conceptually, what we're saying is that a city's health and vitality lies in this overlap between how you balance the needs of the economy, the community, and the natural environment."

The vision, then, is to reconnect downtown with the river and the community on the other side. While efforts continue to develop housing, business, entertainment, and retail in the city center, much is now also happening along the river's edge.

Here are a few certainties and some possibilities, moving east to west. At the southern terminus of the Robert Street Bridge, the new U.S. Bancorp support facility will be humming with the activity of 2,400 employees, with up to 1,000 units of housing nearby. Passing beneath the Wabasha Bridge, the rehabilitation of Raspberry Island beneath the span will have turned this long-ignored little isle into a lovely spot for urban picnicking and entertainment events. On the downtown side of the bridge is the Ramsey County Adult Detention Center, which houses some of the nation's luckiest prisoners, whose cells have beautiful southern views of the river valley. Plans are currently being formulated to move this function elsewhere, and make the site—with the jail either retrofitted or removed—suitable for more law-abiding citizens. Possibilities include housing or a hotel.

Farther west, an urban village along the once-desolate Upper Landing will be complete. The old Shepard Road running nearby will have been converted by 2003 into a bike and walking trail along river's edge, with connections to the River Road paths and the Gateway Trail to Stillwater.

Elsewhere on the river, a floating restaurant on the public dock opened during the summer of 2001. The following summer, a floating theater managed by the University of Minnesota's Theater Department will commence performances. The "head house," the old remnant grain elevator on the Upper Landing, will most likely be redeveloped in some way. Throughout the valley in the downtown area, Seeb and others envision "small, entrepreneurial businesses that start opening up to take advantage of the number of people living here, the number of people who are coming back."

Then there is the very special area called the West Side Flats, just south of downtown.

For those not familiar with the many geographic peculiarities of St. Paul, the "West Side" is actually south of downtown. During much of the 20th century, the West Side Flats flood plain stretching from the river to the bluffs was home to waves of immigrants who landed in St. Paul and settled there. The community between the bluffs and the river, while generally impoverished, was also lively and vigorous. The residents drew from this energy and sense of community many times, particularly during the spring, when the river often rose over its banks and flooded the area's streets under several feet of water. By the late 1950s, the city, working through the St. Paul Port Authority, decided that the Flats (like the "Levee," the mostly Italian settlement on the Upper Landing, and "Swede Hollow" east of downtown) had outlived its residential usefulness, and its houses and most of its streets were cleared away. The people who lived there, mostly ethnic Mexicans, moved primarily inland to the Concord/Robert confluence or up on the bluffs. Much to their chagrin, flood walls and other protections were then put into place, and the area given over primarily to industrial uses.

By the 1990s, much of that industry had closed up or moved, and the Flats area had become desolate and underused. This kind of decay is by no means unique to St. Paul. As American river cities developed, the riparian banks were typically lined with industrial structures—flour mills, factories, and warehouses. The

reason is obvious: Riverside locations made it easier for these facilities to transport their goods to distant markets. As rail lines
were built, they too were often clustered beside the river in order
to serve the businesses that were already in place. These days, of
course, industry no longer relies on riverboats and trains to move
its goods. Nor, by and large, does it require great brick factories
and warehouses. And on the Flats, many of these structures are
gone, and many of the rail lines have been pulled up. But while
there has been some redevelopment, much of the land remains
desolate.

The redevelopment of the Upper Landing, the rejuvenation of
Harriet and Raspberry Islands, and the U.S. Bancorp facility at
the Robert Street bridgehead, will do much to stimulate further
reclamation of land on both sides of the river. The Riverfront
Corp. is promoting the idea of more residential construction on
the West Side Flats toward the bluffs and the Del Sol neighborhood around Robert and Concord Streets. It also would like to
see removal of more of the remaining railroad tracks. While
these tracks are still being used, the trains that use them may be
rerouted around the central district.

Compared to all that has happened downtown, the process of
reclaiming the Flats as a residential neighborhood will be grad-
ual. The efforts of the Capital City Partnership, the Riverfront
Corp., and its partners could be described as centrifugal— "from
the middle outwards," in the words of Seeb. As the "revisioning"
continues downtown, the notion is that the momentum will
spread farther and farther out.

One concept that would help achieve this is a proposed new
stadium for the St. Paul Saints minor league baseball team. The
Saints, which have enjoyed a remarkable success attracting fans
since their inaugural season in 1993, have played home games at
Midway Stadium, a city-owned facility near the state fairgrounds.
Midway's small scale has been a big part of the charm of the
modern-day Saints' contests.

But there are some disadvantages to the current site, which is why the team has approached the city to build a new park. Built in the 1970s, Midway Stadium seats 6,300. There are no luxury suites, and there are limited points of sale for food and merchandise. What's more, the area around Midway Stadium is largely industrial, or simply not conducive to further "city-building." Nor is it a "destination," where people can gather before or after a game.

From a developmental standpoint, then, it would make far more sense to put a new Saints ballpark in the city center. One location that the city has proposed is an open area on the West Side just south of Harriet Island. This placement would put the Saints right near downtown, but would still allow the team enough open area nearby for parking. The proposed stadium would seat 7,500, and would include 26 suites, as well as many more locations for food and merchandise sales. At the same time, this new stadium would bring about a half-million people into downtown annually. Thus, the stadium's proximity to both downtown and the West Side Flats could help stimulate further development of restaurants and other entertainment venues in the immediate area, as well as the creation of even more housing.

In addition, this proposed stadium site also would be facing the Xcel Energy Center just across the river. These two sports/entertainment venues could, in a sense, tie both sides of the river together more firmly, linked by the Wabasha Bridge. As of this writing, the Saints and the city are in discussions regarding the proposal.

A new Saints stadium is a field of dreams at this point. But if there's anything that Norm Coleman and the Capital City Partnership have proved over the past five years, it's that dreams do have a way have coming true. Their success is very largely due to an interfusing of the visionary and the practical. The visions of the mayor, the Capital City Partnership, the Riverfront Corp., and their various allies have imagined aren't castles in the air, but have, in a sense, been built on solid ground.

And that ground is the city as it really is. Downtown St. Paul is easy to get around because it is not big. Its buildings are not tall by modern urban-American norms. Its streets are narrower, its blocks are shorter. St. Paul's downtown is much easier to get around by foot. In the words of Capital City Partnership CEO Labosky, "Think of the warmth and intimacy of the Ordway Center as opposed to the cool modernism of Orchestra Hall [in Minneapolis]."

That sentence boils down the appeal of St. Paul. It has an intimacy reminiscent of smaller European cities like Stuttgart or Strasbourg. St. Paul is a "big" city, but not an overwhelming one, and its density is much more manageable than most "major-league" American cities. Getting around on foot or by car is far less of a challenge. And that has been goal of the mayor and the Capital City Partnership: to capitalize on downtown St. Paul's geographic strengths, rather than to make it into something that it is not and never has been. The idea is to create a richer symphony of buildings, streets, and people. This should be a strolling city, the true center of the community. This is a vision of a city center beyond giant glass towers and streets more friendly to automobiles than to pedestrians. "A city on a human scale" is the phrase you often hear inside City Hall and the offices of the Capital City Partnership.

And that vision is what makes downtown St. Paul, whatever its past difficulties, a city of the future. In the past 10 years, Americans have fallen in love with cities again. They are moving back into the city center to live by the thousands. This trend means that St. Paul is well-positioned to become the kind of distinctive, people-friendly urban community that people want to live in.

The visionary made real

Throughout his administration, Mayor Coleman has based his visions on what can be achieved. He is, after all, a politician, and the axiom that politics is the art of the possible has a kind of parallel in the efforts of the mayor and his city to rejuvenate St. Paul's center. The men and women who constitute the Capital

City Partnership are all builders—builders of businesses. But at the same time, they too have the practicality of politicians; they are able to work with others, pushing where they can, bending where they need to. And in order to overcome years of near-stultification, the rebirth of downtown St. Paul needed the efforts of people who could push, and push hard, lest the necessary changes not take place, and lest the ensuing momentum get derailed. A combination of the visionary and practical, then, has been at the heart of the Capital City Partnership's success, and of the mayor's as well.

Without a doubt, downtown St. Paul has made great strides over the past six years. And it's equally indubitable that Mayor Coleman and the Partnership have provided the energy and vision to make those giant steps possible. But even the rejuvenated city core's most fervent boosters acknowledge that however far St. Paul has come, it still has far to go. There are still too many empty storefronts, too many streets with too few pedestrians, too many underutilized buildings. Even successful structures, such as the lovely old Landmark Center, one of the architectural jewels facing Rice Park, can often seem cavernous, despite the fact that it houses the Minnesota Museum of American Art. The conditions that will generate a critical mass of office workers and residents the vigorous street life, the buzz of conversation and the rhythm of footsteps are still being built, and envisioned.

Like the reopening of the Union Depot as a working train station, many of these visions are more dreams than firm plans at least for now. And that fact leads to another concern: Given how far downtown St. Paul has come under the leadership of Mayor Coleman, many people are wondering what will happen after he leaves office. In an October 2001 interview, Brian Sweeney, the head of the city's Planning & Economic Development department, said that "the next mayor will be a housing mayor." But that would not have been likely if Norm Coleman, along with the Capital City Partnership he created, had not envisioned a city center rich with residential development.

The Grand Excursion will mark the halfway point of the city's 20-year project to transform St. Paul from a dowdy dowager to a vibrant urbanite. Among its other goals, the Excursion is intended to keep up the momentum and excitement that has stimulated downtown St. Paul's remarkable turnaround. But as city leaders have noted, 20 years is a long time, and the various developmental agencies involved—the Riverfront Corp., the Port Authority, Planning & Economic Development, and the Capital City Partnership—know that maintaining something of Norm Coleman's vision and his tirelessness as both leader and salesman over a such a time span will be a particular challenge.

Still, while these efforts will lose much with Coleman's departure, it's important to remember that most of the other players will still be in place. All are witnesses to what can be achieved, and what is possible. "The big change that's occurring is the level of confidence that people have in St. Paul and the future," notes Seeb. "The new buildings are simply a manifestation of that confidence. It's amazing how that spirit of confidence becomes self-fulfilling."

Pointing to the fact that several large business entities have expanded their presence in downtown in the past five years, Labosky says that "the board of directors of the Capital City Partnership believe that we have to take an even stronger role in the future with the new mayor. The private sector is going to have to continue to step up and form an effective partnership with the public sector. Mayor Coleman has done a great job at establishing this urban master plan and creating the great positive momentum that this city has. And we're going to figure out how we can continue that positive momentum. It's going to be a challenge, but I think that we can do it.

"I believe that one of the tests of Mayor Coleman's leadership is how well we're going to do after he's gone," Labosky adds. "Because if you're really a leader, you establish a broader base of leaders who can in fact carry on and make things better when you leave. And so I think we'll be just fine."

It's highly unlikely that the CEOs who make up the member-ship of the Capital City Partnership, nor the citizens and the po-litical leadership of St. Paul, would welcome the return of the sluggishness of the 1980s and early 1990s. But as far the continua-tion of the city center's renaissance is concerned, that train has already left the station.

Q&A: Norm Coleman

St. Paul's outgoing mayor discusses the key points in St. Paul's revitalization—and how they grew out of a shared vision for the city.

BY TOM MASON

On the day that Randy Kelly was elected to be the next mayor of St. Paul, I visited Norm Coleman for a quick discussion of his eight years as mayor. Not to talk about the chronology of events during his tenure, which have been amply covered in this book— but to share his insights about how the inter-relatedness of certain "plot points" in St. Paul's revitalization were connected to his overall vision—and how it all adds up to the economic legacy he bequeaths to Kelly and the people of St. Paul.

Mason: When you first declared your candidacy for mayor, St. Paul was a fairly depressed place, both economically and emotionally. It did not feel good about itself or its prospects. What made you think you could make a difference?

Coleman: David Ben Gurion, the first prime minister of Israel, said, "Anyone who does not believe in miracles is not a realist." I believe in miracles. I'm a realist. I believed that St. Paul could be a much better city. I couldn't have predicted what actually has happened, but I always knew, in my gut, we could bring it back to being a great big small town.

Mason: At one point of personal enlightenment did you see the Mississippi River as the common dominator of your economic vision for the city?

Coleman: There wasn't a single moment, rather a confluence of two separate factors. On one side, I saw a lot of divisiveness and despair. Our focus groups showed that people in St. Paul were really suffering from a lack of confidence in their economic future, even a lack of hope. About that same time, I was talking to people like Paul Verret at the St. Paul Foundation and Dick Broeker, who saw great potential on the river and made it come alive for me. I'm a great believer that when you get people fired up about something, there will be an overflow effect. If I rallied folks around the river, I would have the capacity to improve the economic piece. It was making the linkage between two very separate concepts that ultimately came together.

Mason: Some of your friends say that you sustained some pretty harsh political beatings that first year, especially from commercial real estate people who were particularly hurting. They didn't want vision. They wanted tenants.

Coleman: It wasn't a case of getting beat up. It was a case of total rejection of the vision by certain stakeholders. But once you make up your mind on a vision, success is a matter of staying focused and persevering. I was getting heat on other issues. For example, when I was informed that we had $200 million in unfounded liability for retiree health benefits, I decided to reject the AFSME contract. Almost all my advisors and key staff said, "Mayor, don't do that. It's political suicide. That's the next mayor's problem." I decided we had to take it on. I wasn't willing to see the city in bankruptcy in 15 years—even if it would be the next mayor's problem.

We got sued. We got picketed. It got ugly. But that was a tougher battle. Some people thought I was crazy. The unions got all fired up. Some of my good friends and supporters in the fire department were up in arms. But it was that move that in many ways solidified my relationship with the business community. I don't think I'd have a Capital City Partnership if I hadn't fought that battle.

I also remember bringing in all my department heads the first year and saying, "We're not going to raise taxes and we're going to keep a lid on spending." Almost every one of them asked for an increase in their budgets. I chuckled and asked a couple of them, "What are you doing?" They said, "Everyone always says that." It was almost Pavlovian.

So, I'm fighting the battle for fiscal responsibility at the same time I'm trying to weave a positive vision for how to pull people together. And the two came together.

Mason: You invested a lot of time on developing personal relationships with business leaders.

Coleman: After I got elected, one of the first things I did was go to Doug Leatherdale at The St. Paul Companies and to Desi Desimone at 3M, and a few others. I asked for advice on running a large operation: How do I run a business of 3000 employees? They talked to me about having a core vision of where you want to go and what you want to accomplish. About motivating people to get their focus—they talked a lot about focus. I don't think they had had a politician come to them and ask, "How do you do what you do well? How do run a city like a successful business."

Mason: Ecolab and Minnesota Life gave you a very important early victory when they decided to expand in their downtown locations, rather than following West Publishing to the suburbs or, worse, outside of Minnesota. How much did you fear their potential departures and how valuable was it that they stayed?

Coleman: In the early days the fear was very real. The joke was that Doug Leatherdale and The St. Paul Companies would be the last folks to turn out the lights in downtown St. Paul. It was absolutely critical that they stayed. They had to stay. Ecolab had to expand here, not in Tennessee or somewhere else.

I had the sense of what St. Paul could be, but it wasn't there yet. It took leaps of faith on the part of Al Schuman at Ecolab or Bob Senkler at Minnesota Life. I knew Al Schuman. I spent time with him. These are friends with whom I developed relationships. You sit down and break bread with them. So that when the time comes that you have to ask for something, you aren't the detached politician coming in from city hall—you are someone with a connection.

Mason: The nexus of your relationships with CEOs seemed to culminate with the creation of the Capital City Partnership.

Coleman: There was important symbolism in getting a commitment from folks at the highest levels of business to be involved in the future of St. Paul. The vision of that is magnificent. The reality is even better. When CEOs are involved all manner of great things can happen.

The practical reality is that the mayor can't do things alone. All of a sudden I have huge allies in John Labosky and the members of the Capital City Partnership. I also have a Chamber of Commerce growing and providing great leadership under Larry Dowell.

Mason: You once said that there was only one person you wanted to run the Capital City Partnership and that was John Labosky.

Coleman: I can't say that was all my work. Peter Ridder [former publisher of the *St. Paul Pioneer Press*] played a role with that, as did Doug Leatherdale. John has great relationships with all of the corporate community. He knew what it takes to market and promote a city. He has a legal background. He knows design, as the former CEO of Ellerbe-Becket. Recruiting John to head the organization while we were forming the Capital City Partnership happened hand in hand.

Mason: Your riverfront approach seemed to gain great credibility when the St. Paul Chamber Orchestra gave its now-famous concert-on-a-barge on the Mississippi. You expected to draw 2,000 people, you got 8,000. Was this a point at which your critics started to soften?

Coleman: I think it had that impact. I recall that an editorial in the *Star Tribune* raised the stakes the day before the event by asking, "Will they come?" They did.

People often need to see or physically experience something before they get excited about it. I always knew that. It is why we always try to create visual, tangible things that people can tap into. My belief was that if we finally get folks down to the river, great things would happen. Lawson Software was a liability until people saw the building. The riverfront was an abstract vision until people could come down and experience it.

Mason: What would have happened if only 1,000 people showed up?

Coleman: We would have come up with another idea. We would have brought them down the next week for something else. You have to believe in the vision and stay with it. Individual things don't always work out. If one door shuts, you walk around and try another one, until you find one that works.

Mason: The Science Museum of Minnesota's new building brought a lot of attention and prestige to the city. Some observers say that your ability to persuade museum leaders to locate on the downtown side of the river was essential to connecting the downtown to the Mississippi. I've heard at least person suggest that this victory changed your management style—that you became a more confident manager who was actually "putting pieces together, not just hoping that they fell in the right place." Do you agree?

Coleman: It is not about management. It is about seeing the whole and how the pieces fit together. There could have been a great Science Museum on the west side of St. Paul, with a suburban design. But our vision was clear: We wanted something that would connect the downtown with the river. The question was: How do we make it happen?

I remember having a conversation with Dick Broeker, just before a meeting with [Science Museum President] Jim Peterson, thinking, "How do we make him an offer he can't refuse?" We figured this was $90 million deal—half public, half private. We figured the state could do twice what we could do—and we came up with $15 million. I couldn't even tell you where it was coming from at the time. We knew it would be an offer they couldn't refuse—but we also knew it did what we could to make the museum what we needed it to be.

It was a never a function of, "Here's the money, go play." It was a matter of we had a vision, so that if folks had a design concept that didn't fit the vision, we had a place at the table.

I try not to micromanage, but I also try to be clear about what we need. A big part of my job is to pull those pieces together, whether that means the financial piece, for the Science Museum or working on the design side.

Mason: The decision by Lawson Software to relocate its 1000

153

employees to a gleaming new headquarters in downtown St. Paul marks another turning point, especially when you consider it had been located in downtown Minneapolis's back yard. How do you place it among the building blocks for St. Paul?

Coleman: When I finally thought we were close to having the Lawson piece done, I still needed help filling the space. So I called Doug Leatherdale at home on a Friday night. Doug said, "This is more significant than the Wild—1,000 jobs, downtown. Make it happen. I'll do what I have to do."

My job is to keep the deals together. Other people do the economics or the deal points or negotiate. Without them it wouldn't happen. My job is to figure out how to keep it alive, so that in the end we keep it going.

Mason: How important was the task of keeping Dayton's (now Marshall Fields) from closing its downtown store?

Coleman: Keeping Dayton's was more than a defensive move. It has transformed into a tremendous positive affirmation. If it had left, it would have been a disaster. Dayton's is an icon. Keeping it in St. Paul was essential. The fact that it stayed was an affirmation of all the other things going on. It was a response to Lawson, to riverfront development. Early on, Target President Bob Ulrich questioned whether all this would happen. Today he is a firm believer and a magnificent cheerleader for St. Paul.

Mason: The biggest success story, if only for its improbability, was in attracting the Wild, St. Paul's NHL franchise. You have called it a deal that survived a hundred near-death experiences because it was destined to happen. Did that symbolize the inevitability of St. Paul's comeback or was it just luck.

Coleman: Maybe a little of both. Things don't happen on their own. This was not a stone rolling down a hill. It wouldn't have happened if [Wild CEO] Jac Sperling or [owner] Bob Naegele or [former Planning & Economic Development director] Pam Wheelock or Norm Coleman hadn't been there. But the fact is we were all there and we all played our part. I believe God puts us in the position to get things done. We had the right people at the right time in the right place with the right vision—and the right ability to make the vision come alive.

Mason: When you sat down with your friends after you knew the Wild would be a reality, did you think it was your most satisfying accomplishment?

Coleman: As tough as Lawson or others had been, this one was so unlikely, you almost had to laugh. At times, we were bluffing. We put together an ownership group and submitted an application to the NHL—and we didn't have a firm dollar commitment from anybody. We didn't have the money for a deposit. We didn't have a lead investor until the day before we actually needed one. Along the way, there was a lot of smoke and mirrors, but we knew we had the right vision, we knew it would be good for St. Paul.

Even afterward, I don't think we understood how great it would be. Clearly, the Wild have created something remarkable. For me, it didn't really sink in until opening night, or maybe it the day Wild beat Dallas at home.

Mason: Would you agree that Norm Coleman's legacy to St. Paul is in bringing back its self-confidence? St. Paul now says to business, "You need to be here, for the sake of your business,"— not, "We need you to be here for the sake of St. Paul."

Coleman: St. Paul today is a very attractive place for a lot of reasons. But it is so in part because we created a shared vision among the government, the business community, and the foundation community about who we are and what we can be. It is not something we created out of thin air. It represented a shared vision that we are a great big small town. We are a safe community. We are a place where people know each other. We are a great place to raise kids, to create jobs, and to retire. It's what most places in America want to be—it is what St. Paul is.